Lee Bailey's
Cooking
for
Friends

LEE BAILEY'S
COOKING FOR FRIENDS

by Lee Bailey

Photographs by Tom Eckerle

Design by Impress

Recipe Testing and
Development with Lee Klein

GRAMERCY BOOKS
New York

This 1998 edition is published by
Gramercy Books®, a division of
Random House Value Publishing, Inc.,
by arrangement with Clarkson N. Potter,
a member of the Crown Publishing Group,
201 East 50th Street, New York, NY 10022.

Printed in China.

Gramercy Books® and design
are registered trademarks of
Random House Value Publishing, Inc.

**Library of Congress
Cataloging-in-Publication Data**
Bailey, Lee.
Lee Bailey's cooking for friends/by Lee Bailey;
photographs by Tom Eckerle; design by
Impress; recipe testing and development
with Lee Klein.
p. cm.
Originally published: New York: C. Potter,
1992.
Includes index.
ISBN 0-517-20307-3
1. Cookery, International.   I. Title.
TX725.A1B265 1998
641.59—dc21 97-51779
CIP

Random House
New York • Toronto • London
Sydney • Auckland
http://www.randomhouse.com/

CONTENTS

ACKNOWLEDGMENTS

A SPECIAL THANK YOU to all my dedicated friends at Clarkson Potter for doing their usual terrific job. And ditto to Tom Eckerle, Hans Teensma, Pam Bernstein, and Lee Klein.

In Key West, my appreciation to Anthony Childs; Joshua Greene and Soffie Kage; Bill Halpin; Carolyn Holloway; David and Lynn Kaufelt; Roberta Lowe; Polly Porter; Susan Rogers; Waterside Fish Market, John Peck, Dale and Bichon Applegate; Stephen Widup; and Dana Wilson.

In Greece, my appreciation to Stefano and Caliope Baha; Peter Bacanovic; Grazia Gazzoni; Sherwin Goldman; Irene, Victor, and Nicky Gouras; Ashton Hawkins; and Tim Husband.

In Tuscany, my appreciation to Adriana; Joe Allen; Daniela Bondi, Silvestro Baraldo, and Emanuela at the Bar Centrale; Cipriani; and Bruce and Laurie Wolf.

In Gascony, my appreciation to Bridgit and Jean-Marc Duarte; Alain Garcia; and Dagmar and Walter Sullivan.

In Bridgehampton, my appreciation to Peachy Halsey and her crew and Fleurette Guilloz.

In New York City, my appreciation to D. D. Allen, Vinnie Arbona, Tom Booth, Christian Breschneff, Joel Dean, Amy Gross, Perry Guillot, Tim Lovejoy, Fern Mallis, Grace Monroe, Louis Porco, and Helen Skor.

In St. Barth's, my appreciation to Brooke and Roger Lacour and Eric Lamb.

INTRODUCTION

OR YEARS NOW I've had a habit that friends like to tease me about. You see, it seems that almost every time I tell someone about a new dish, I'll say it's a particular favorite of mine. I know these friends are right, I've even caught myself saying it. But I really mean it. It just so happens I've lots of particular favorites, that's all. And, if anyone is especially complimentary about something we've had at dinner, I'm likely to print out the recipe for them right then (everything's in the trusty old word processor now). I get ribbed about that, too.

So a few years ago I found myself with lots of recipes, menus, and dishes that I'd discovered or developed — recipes that had become "favorites" of mine but that had never been in any of my books. You can imagine how frustrated I felt. And in looking over this information all together I realized I'd expanded my horizons, adding new elements and exploring other methods. For instance, I had not only started serving soups as a main course (which I wrote about in

Soup Meals), but I had also started experimenting with more kinds of pastas, desserts, salads, and simple cuts of meat that could be quickly cooked and easily served. Underneath it all I'm still the same home-cooking kid, but by simply doing what comes naturally, I think I've revitalized some old favorites, learned some useful new things, and in the process given myself a lift.

What this adds up to is, I've got lots of stuff and thoughts I've been squirreling away that I want to tell you about. So here it is, friends — the new, up-to-date, old Bailey for the first part of the 90s.

The other aspect of this book — the various locations where we cooked and photographed — was not just a cute trick to find pretty places to take pictures (although there is nothing wrong with that "in my books"). Maybe the best way to explain is to tell this little story on myself. Sometime just after the mid-60s, it seemed that every other day I'd hear of someone I knew who was planning a move to London. The mod scene was in full swing there and the place seemed both jazzier and more civilized than New York. Although I was getting a little long in the tooth to be part of any mod scene, something about all this activity got to me, and I began carry-

ing on about how I was going to leave New York for some better, as yet undetermined, spot. My destination changed regularly, and in truth it had never been really clear in my head.

Then, after about six months of boring everyone practically senseless with my complaining and pipe dreams, came an evening when I found myself having a nightcap with an old friend and her husband. It must have been a balmy night as we were at an outdoor café on Fifth Avenue looking across toward the Metropolitan Museum. I suppose I'd behaved during dinner, but by the time our after-dinner drinks arrived I was off onto my litany. I paused to take a breath, and my friend seized the moment to say — with an ever-so-faint smile that took the curse off — "Will you shut up!" That stopped me. She'd never, even jokingly, rebuked me so flatly. I knew she was serious, maybe more so than she even knew. Before I could respond, she went on to say, "The point is you can't live any place *but* New York. You *need* the city to work in, and you've been here long enough now so that it needs you in a way. So why don't you make peace with it and give us all a break?" Then we all had a bit of a laugh.

I woke up the following morning and started to think clearly and seriously about what I did and — more important — did not like about New York City. And first was the fact that, as seductive as the place can be, living here full time, all the time, was awfully tough on the nerves.

Fortunately, I already had my house in the country, but now I had to figure

a way to work out there in the warm months. Being self-employed helped, and by 1969 I made plans with a partner to open a sort of "sell anything" design store in Southampton. Over time this led to my shop at Bendel's and when that was sold, to Saks. It also spun off my writing career.

But getting scraps of relief from the city's pressures was only half the problem. The other thing was — and is — that it's really hard for me to endure cold weather. Being from the South, I think my poor old body still hopes and thinks spring weather will start to settle in around the beginning of March. All these years notwithstanding, I can only take it up through January because the fall is so very exhilarating and I love the action that continues through the holidays and a little beyond, but after that all I dream of is escape. So escape I did. I realized I needed a vacation more in February than I ever did during warm weather, so I switched my free time to winter. This is when I started renting houses on various islands — single-o and with groups of friends. Later on we moved to other parts of the world, and over time I learned to work out of my suitcase.

So you see, it isn't so farfetched for me to be cooking for friends in kitchens other than my own.

Another interesting thing about this vagabond cooking is that by adapting my basic recipes to local ingredients and popular methods of doing things I've often found ways that are even more pleasing than the "originals."

Of course, cooking in a strange kitchen has its drawbacks and perils, but I got accustomed to improvising with what was at hand. Besides, my pattern was

to keep returning to a place I liked so I was better prepared the second time around. And with experience, I learned what questions to ask when I was renting someplace new. Questions like, How many pots and pans are provided? Is there a blender? Is there something to grill food on? What foods are generally available at the local markets?

When we started following the sun, places like St. Martin were still pretty primitive by today's standards. On our first visit, owing to the shortage of decent fresh meat, poultry, and salad greens, we had to drag (literally) along a locker of frozen meats, as well as heads of iceberg lettuce, which stayed usable for up to a couple of weeks when refrigerated. And speaking of the refrigerator, island electricity can be very antic so we had to become accustomed to its vagaries.

Here is probably the place to add a little tip. It might seem rather inconsequential, but think about it. In with the books I always take along insect repellent, sun block, film, and such — plus a small knife sharpener and an oven thermometer. As a renter, I've encountered more dull knives than you can shake a carrot at and about as many unreliable ovens, both of which can drive you crazy when you are trying to work with the typical minimally equipped kitchen you'll find in most rented vacation houses. Of course, such aggravations could be avoided altogether by staying at a hotel, but I've personally never liked that as well as being in a private house.

As I write about this I find I smile remembering the pleasures I've had. Now that I'm often gone (with the wind?), living in New York City is a breeze.

In the Keys

VISITING THE FLORIDA KEYS is almost like going home to my childhood. For although I grew up in central Louisiana, every summer we would go down to Grande Isle, a big island in the Gulf just off the coast where the marshlands give way to open water. There my cousins and I would gorge ourselves on shrimp and oysters, exhaust ourselves in the gentle, shallow surf, get sunburned, and be bitten by mosquitoes. It was great.

In those days you could stand chest deep in the water with nets attached to poles stuck in the sandy bottom and catch big blue crabs as fast as you could haul the nets in. Then down by the docks, when the fishing boats came in with the day's catch, you had your choice from piles of giant shrimp, great baskets of oysters, and all manner of Gulf fish. In the early evenings sometimes there'd be shrimp or crab boils where a big washtub filled with shrimp or crabs and heavily spiced water would be set to cooking outside over a fire laid in a pit. When the seafood was done, it was drained and allowed to cool. Meanwhile, tops of the long trestle tables on the screened-in porches would be covered with newspaper. Then at suppertime metal trays would be heaped with seafood and set out with lemon wedges and bowls of catsup and horseradish sauce, and everyone would dive in, kids and grownups alike. We kids would peel and eat and make such a mess that we would almost have to be hosed down. Afterwards, all the shells, squeezed lemon halves, and sauce drippings would be folded up in the newspapers and thrown out. This wasn't about style; it was about eating, plain and simple. But now that I think about it, the whole thing did have its own kind of style.

I've since wondered if my parents and their friends knew how wonderful those summers were. Almost all of them are gone now. I certainly hope they did.

ABOVE: *Ixora.*
OPPOSITE: *Residence of interior decorator Antony Childs.*

Well, I guess I can't pretend lots hasn't happened in the decades since those long-past summers with their seemingly endless days, but the Gulf seafood is still there, and the shallow surf is still there. And there are even a few mosquitoes.

Nowadays planning meals in such places is certainly more a matter of making choices than of making do (as you often must in Greece or the Caribbean). All the basics are available, even those that only a short time ago were considered exotic. However, since the seafood and fish are so plentiful here, that's what I like to concentrate on, especially if I know my visit is going to be a brief one.

But I've got to admit that as tantalizing as the memory of those piles of shrimp and crabs waiting to be peeled is, I don't try to re-create such meals. There are still restaurants with big screened-in porches, particularly along the more rural stretches of the Gulf, where you can indulge in seafood orgies. And it's especially nice if you can find one where you can run out into the surf to wash off and cool down afterwards.

By the Pool

ONE OF THE BEST THINGS about planning lunches in the Keys is that there is so much fresh produce to choose from. We don't do too much real cooking for noon-time meals — raw fruits and vegetables simply dressed or marinated, accompanied by make-ahead dishes, are our choice. As a matter of fact, this is not so very different from what I always do when I'm planning hot weather lunches anywhere.

OPPOSITE: *A spray of frangipani.*
BELOW: *A serving of Avocados with Lime Vinaigrette, Marinated Mushrooms, Sliced Tomatoes, and the Shrimp, Crab, and Gulf Fish Salad.* RIGHT: *Palms along the beach.*

SHRIMP, CRAB, AND GULF FISH SALAD

SLICED TOMATOES WITH LEMON JUICE

MARINATED MUSHROOMS

AVOCADOS WITH LIME VINAIGRETTE

CRUSTY ROLLS WITH TABASCO BUTTER

LIME ICE CREAM

TROPICAL FRUIT COMPOTE

SHRIMP, CRAB, AND GULF FISH SALAD

Now I ask you, who doesn't love seafood salad? And almost any medley of local catch suffices. In this case we used shrimp, crab meat, and a member of the snapper family found in the Gulf and referred to locally as "hogfish."

- 1 pound medium shrimp, peeled, deveined, and boiled in heavily spiced water (see *Note*)
- 1 pound back-fin lump crab meat, picked over
- 1 pound mild firm white fish, poached in a rich court-bouillon (recipe follows)
- 2 generous tablespoons capers
- ¼ generous cup coarsely chopped dill pickle
- 1 large fennel bulb, trimmed, with core out, cut into medium slices
- 6 generous tablespoons medium diced red onion

VINAIGRETTE

- 2 tablespoons minced red onion
- 2 tablespoons minced fresh dill
- 1 tablespoon minced dill pickle
- 2 teaspoons minced capers
- ¼ cup olive oil
- 2 teaspoons caper juice
- 2 tablespoons red wine vinegar
- ½ teaspoon black pepper
- ¾ teaspoon salt
- 4 dashes Tabasco

Place whole shrimp, flaked crab meat, and white fish — broken into bite-size pieces — in a mixing bowl. Toss with the capers, pickle, fennel, and onion. Set aside, covered, in the refrigerator.

Make the vinaigrette.

Place minced onion, dill, pickle, and capers in a small bowl. Whisk together the olive oil, caper juice, vinegar, pepper, salt, and Tabasco. Pour over minced ingredients and mix well.

When ready to serve, toss the vinaigrette with the seafood and fish.
Serves 8

Note: In the South most people use a commercial shrimp or crab boil mix composed of herbs and hot spices. Check your specialty store.

COURT-BOUILLON

You can cover shrimp peelings with water, simmer for 10 minutes, and use the resulting liquid to enhance this stock.

- 1 cup dry white wine
  Juice of ½ lemon
- 2 medium carrots, scraped and thinly sliced
- 1 medium onion, chopped
- 2 celery ribs, thinly sliced
- 1 bay leaf
- 2 quarts water

Combine all ingredients in a stock pot with water. Bring slowly to a boil and simmer 30 minutes. Court-bouillon is ready for poaching fish. Add desired fish and simmer for about 10 minutes per inch of thickness.
Makes 3 quarts

SLICED TOMATOES WITH LEMON JUICE

If I had to choose just one way to eat tomatoes, I think my choice would be to simply top them with freshly squeezed lemon juice about 30 minutes prior to serving, with maybe a grind of black pepper (and salt if you like).

MARINATED MUSHROOMS

These should be served at room temperature.

- 1 pound white mushrooms, brushed clean
- ¼ cup plus 2 tablespoons olive oil
- ½ cup finely chopped shallots
- 2 heaping tablespoons minced garlic
- 3 tablespoons fresh lemon juice
- ½ cup dry white wine
- 1¾ cups chicken stock
- 1 large bay leaf
- ½ teaspoon crushed coriander seeds
- ½ teaspoon crushed black peppercorns
- ¼ teaspoon paprika
- 1 tablespoon chopped fresh thyme

Separate the mushroom caps from the stems and set caps aside. Coarsely chop the stems.

In a nonreactive skillet, heat ¼ cup of the olive oil and sauté the shallots over medium-high heat, tossing, until they begin to brown very lightly, about 5 minutes. Add the mushroom stems and continue to cook, stirring occasionally, until they give off their liquid and start to turn golden, about 15 to 20 minutes.

Add the garlic to the mushrooms and cook another minute or so, stirring. Add the lemon juice, wine, and 1½ cups stock. Bring to a boil and add spices. Stir to deglaze pan. Turn heat back to a simmer and add mushroom caps. Poach 2 to 3 minutes, until tender. Remove with a slotted spoon and set aside.

Reduce poaching liquid over medium-high heat until almost all has evaporated, about 20 to 25 minutes. Whisk in the remaining olive oil and the remaining ¼ cup of heated chicken stock. Pour over caps and toss. Refrigerate, covered, overnight. Bring to room temperature before serving.
Serves 6

AVOCADOS WITH LIME VINAIGRETTE

If you are rushed (or simply would rather swim than cook), a simple oil and vinegar dressing would be fine on avocados. Or if you are really a minimalist, just add a squeeze of lemon or lime juice. Whatever you do, rub the cut surfaces of avocado with citrus juice to keep them from discoloring before being served.

¼ cup olive oil
2 tablespoons fresh lime juice
1 tablespoon mayonnaise
3 to 4 dashes Tabasco (optional)
1 teaspoon Dijon-style mustard
½ teaspoon salt, or to taste
½ teaspoon black pepper
2 tablespoons minced shallots
3 tablespoons finely chopped sweet red pepper
3 ripe avocados, peeled, pitted, and quartered

In a small glass bowl, whisk together the olive oil and lime juice. Whisk in mayonnaise, Tabasco, and mustard. Mix in salt and pepper, then fold in shallots and red pepper.

To serve, drizzle over prepared avocado quarters.

Makes about ¾ cup vinaigrette

———

CRUSTY ROLLS WITH TABASCO BUTTER

Tabasco butter, popular throughout the southern part of the country, is made by whipping as much Tabasco as you think you can handle into softened sweet butter.

Incidentally, Tabasco butter is good to use when making garlic bread. Gives it an added kick.

LIME ICE CREAM

I don't make ice cream unless I have an automatic machine of some kind. Luckily, this house had one.

⅔ cup sugar
2½ cups half-and-half
5 large egg yolks, at room temperature
  Grated zest of one lemon
½ cup fresh lime juice

Combine the sugar and half-and-half in a large saucepan and cook over low heat until the sugar dissolves, stirring all the while. Set aside.

Beat the egg yolks until creamy, then add ½ cup of the cream mixture to warm them. Return cream mixture to medium-low heat and stir in the warmed yolks. Cook until the mixture coats the back of a spoon, about 5 minutes.

Off the heat, stir in the zest and lime juice. Mix well and allow to cool. Chill.

Pour mixture into an ice-cream maker and freeze according to the manufacturer's directions.

Makes about 1½ pints

TROPICAL FRUIT COMPOTE

Use any mélange of fruit you see in the market, but always toss it with the orange juice (unless you are using peeled orange sections in the mixture). I generally make a big batch of this so people can dip into it all day long. Leftovers, if there are any, are fine for breakfast.

3 medium bananas, cut into medium slices
½ medium pineapple, peeled, cored, and cut into small triangles
2 medium papayas, peeled, seeded, and cut into medium chunks
2 large mangos, peeled and cut into chunks
4 kiwi fruits, peeled and cut into thick rings
  Juice of 1 medium orange

Toss all the fruit together with the orange juice. Chill, covered, for just 30 minutes before serving.

If this must wait longer, reserve the bananas until just before serving.

Serves 8 to 10

LEFT: *Lime Ice Cream.*
ABOVE: *Tropical Fruit Compote.*
OVERLEAF: *Key West boats.*

COLD RADISH SOUP

MIXED SEAFOOD CAKES WITH JALAPENO
TARTAR SAUCE AND THIN FRIED ONIONS

CROWDER PEA, BLACK-EYED PEA, AND
BUTTER BEAN SALAD

TOASTED CRACKERS, BUTTERED

PAPAYA, BANANA, AND COCONUT AMBROSIA

On the Porch

THERE ARE TWO particular favorites in this menu: bean salad and seafood cakes. I'm especially fond of the bean salad because it is made with three legumes that are native to the South but that — with the exception of black-eyed peas — are not often available outside the region. So when I saw them in the local market I was delighted. Incidentally, freezing seems to be less harmful to this sturdy group of vegetables than most, so if all you can find in your grocery case are the frozen ones, they will work just fine. However, outside the South even frozen crowder peas and butter beans are difficult to come by.

Seafood cakes seem to be popular with almost everyone. I often make them when I'm in places like the Keys, where seafood and fish are easily available. In truth, many times I make them from leftovers, as I did here. In this case we used shrimp, Gulf lobster, and crab meat. Any assortment will do, but I like to include shrimp.

ABOVE: *Mixed Seafood Cakes and Crowder Pea, Black-Eyed Pea, and Butter Bean Salad.* OPPOSITE: *Bougainvillea.* RIGHT: *View to the back garden.*

COLD RADISH SOUP

Make this as thick or as thin as you choose. You may use either additional chicken stock (which I do), low-fat milk, or light cream. I always make enough of this soup to have leftovers for another meal or an afternoon snack.

- 1 tablespoon unsalted butter
- 1 cup thinly sliced green onions, mostly the white part
- 2 cups small-cubed white potatoes
- 2 cups thinly sliced radishes, plus additional for garnish
- 2⅔ cups chicken stock
- ½ teaspoon white pepper
  Salt (optional)
  Chives for garnish (optional)

Melt butter in a medium saucepan and stir in green onions. Cover tightly and sweat over very low heat about 15 to 20 minutes, until wilted. Do not allow to brown. Add potatoes and radishes and enough chicken stock to cover.

Bring to a boil, turn heat to low, and simmer until potatoes are very tender, about 20 minutes. Place in a food processor and puree until smooth. Return to the saucepan and add the balance of the chicken stock. Add pepper — and salt if your chicken stock had none in it.

Chill and serve with chopped raw radish and snipped chives on top of each serving.
Serves 8 or more

——

MIXED SEAFOOD CAKES WITH JALAPENO TARTAR SAUCE AND THIN FRIED ONIONS

The small batch of fried onions gives the seafood an added lift, but obviously if you don't want to bother with them, don't. However, they *are* worth the effort to me. I prefer the seafood in chunks rather than minced. It allows the individual flavors to come through.

- 4 tablespoons (½ stick) unsalted butter
- ½ cup coarsely chopped onion
- ½ cup coarsely chopped celery
- 2 cups coarsely chopped mixed seafood (such as shrimp, crab meat, lobster, and poached fish, in any proportion)
- 1 tablespoon mayonnaise
- 1 large egg
- 1 tablespoon Worcestershire sauce
- 1 teaspoon dry mustard
- ¼ teaspoon salt
  Dash of black pepper
- ½ teaspoon paprika
- 3 cups fresh, coarse soft bread crumbs
- 2 tablespoons vegetable oil

Heat 1 tablespoon of the butter in a small skillet and sauté the onion and celery over medium heat until wilted, about 5 minutes. Meanwhile, toss together the mixed seafood in a glass bowl. Toss in the wilted onion and celery. In another small glass bowl combine the mayonnaise, egg, Worcestershire sauce,

mustard, salt, pepper, and paprika. Beat with a fork until well mixed. Pour into the seafood and mix lightly. Melt another tablespoon of the butter and pour over all. Mix, being careful not to break up the chunks of crab and fish. Mix in 1 cup of the bread crumbs. Set aside.

Pour the balance of the bread crumbs onto a sheet of waxed paper. Form the seafood mixture into 12 small balls and roll in the crumbs to coat. Place on a plate and flatten slightly. Refrigerate for at least 1 hour.

To cook, heat the vegetable oil and the 2 remaining tablespoons of butter in a large skillet over medium heat. When hot, slide seafood cakes in, being careful not to crowd. After they have cooked for about 30 seconds, flatten and gently loosen them from the bottom of the pan. When golden underneath, about 2 minutes, carefully turn and brown the other side, about 2 minutes. Drain on paper towels.

Serve topped with Thin Fried Onions and Jalapeño Tartar Sauce on the side (recipes follow).
Serves 6

JALEPENO TARTAR SAUCE

1 cup mayonnaise, preferably homemade (page 34)
¼ cup chopped fresh dill
1 medium bottled jalapeño pepper, seeded and minced
3 tablespoons chopped sweet pickles
1 heaping tablespoon small capers
1 tablespoon snipped chives

Mix all ingredients, adding more of any of the ingredients to taste.
Makes about 1¾ cups

THIN FRIED ONIONS

Make these while the seafood cakes are chilling.

1 medium onion
Flour
Vegetable oil for frying
Salt

ABOVE: *Flower-covered gate.* OPPOSITE: *Cold Radish Soup.* OVERLEAF: *Friends at table.*

Peel the onion and cut in half lengthwise. Place flat sides down and slice very thin. Separate and place in a bag with the flour. Shake to coat, then take out and shake off excess flour. Pour about 2 inches of oil into a small pot and heat over high heat. Drop in coated onions and fry very quickly until golden, about 2 minutes. Adjust heat so as not to burn onions. Remove with a slotted spoon and drain on paper towels. Sprinkle with salt.

CROWDER PEA, BLACK-EYED PEA, AND BUTTER BEAN SALAD

Obviously other beans could be substituted for the ones here.

1 cup *each* shelled crowder peas, black-eyed peas, and butter beans
Chicken stock
Salt to taste
1½ cups peeled, seeded, and coarsely chopped tomato
½ cup coarsely chopped celery or jicama
½ cup coarsely chopped red onion
¼ cup olive oil
¼ cup balsamic vinegar

1 tablespoon green peppercorn mustard
1 teaspoon black pepper
3 tablespoons minced shallots

In 3 separate pots, cover the beans with chicken stock, salted to taste, and simmer until tender, about 20 to 25 minutes for the crowders and black-eyed peas, less for the butter beans. Drain and cool. You should save the "pot likker," as the bean cooking liquid is called in South, and use it in soup.

Toss the cooled beans with the tomato, celery or jicama, and red onion. Set aside. In a small bowl combine all other ingredients except the shallots, and whisk. (If you are not planning to serve this immediately, reserve the tomatoes and toss them in just before serving.) Fold in the shallots. Add enough of the dressing to coat the beans.
Serves 6

TOASTED CRACKERS, BUTTERED

Place Saltine crackers on a cookie sheet and run them under the broiler long enough to toast. Butter and set aside.

ABOVE: *Papaya, Banana, and Coconut Ambrosia.* BELOW: *Cuba, Ho!*
RIGHT: *Sunset.*

PAPAYA, BANANA, AND COCONUT AMBROSIA

I'm especially fond of papaya and banana together — and with a sprinkling
of coconut it's even better. Now, if you
are making this far ahead, chill just the
papaya and orange juice mixed. Add
the bananas at the last minute.

2 papayas, peeled, seeded, and
   cut into chunks
2 bananas, peeled and cut into
   thick slices
6 tablespoons fresh orange juice
6 tablespoons or more grated
   fresh coconut

Combine papayas, bananas, and orange
juice. Chill for 30 minutes or more.
Divide among 6 chilled dishes and
sprinkle with coconut.
Serves 6

Sunday Dinner

WE TEND TO HAVE one or two special (in the sense that they are a little more time-consuming to prepare) dinners while we are in residence — what I still call "Sunday Dinners." Some people might find the first course here rather redundant. However, with fish and seafood such a treat in Key West, I don't mind doubling up on it. If you *do* find crab claws a bit too much of a good thing, you could save them to build a lunch around some other day. Whatever you do, don't miss 'em.

OPPOSITE: *Stone Crab Claws with Hot Catsup Mayonnaise.* TOP: *Pink ixora.* ABOVE: *Hibiscus.* BELOW: *Royal poinciana tree.*

STONE CRAB CLAWS WITH HOT CATSUP MAYONNAISE

COLD POACHED GULF FISH WITH
FRESH CUCUMBER SAUCE

RICE, GREEN PEA, AND OLIVE SALAD WITH
ORANGE-CILANTRO VINAIGRETTE

TOASTED THIN-SLICED BREAD AND SWEET BUTTER

COCONUT FLAN

STONE CRAB CLAWS WITH HOT CATSUP MAYONNAISE

Colorful stone crab claws are a staple hereabouts. According to local regulations, they must be cooked before they are sold, so they're an easy first course. Of course, other large crab claws could be substituted. As for the Tabasco, I like this hot.

- 1 cup mayonnaise, preferably homemade (recipe follows)
- 2 tablespoons prepared horseradish
- 1 tablespoon fresh lemon juice
- 1 generous tablespoon catsup
- 4 to 5 dashes Tabasco, or to taste
- 1 teaspoon Dijon-style mustard
- 2 stone crab claws per person

Mix all ingredients but the crab. Serve the hot mayonnaise with crab claws, garnished with lemon wedges.
Makes about 1¼ cups mayonnaise

HOMEMADE MAYONNAISE

- 1 teaspoon dry mustard
- 1 teaspoon salt
  Pinch of black pepper
- 3 tablespoons fresh lemon juice
- 1 large egg
- 1¼ cups vegetable oil
- ¾ cup olive oil
  Dash of Tabasco (optional)

Place mustard, salt, pepper, lemon juice, and egg in a food processor. With the motor running, pour oils in a slow, steady stream through the feed tube until all has been emulsified. Stir in Tabasco.
Makes about 2 cups

———

COLD POACHED GULF FISH WITH FRESH CUCUMBER SAUCE

Choose any firm mild fish for this dish. We used red grouper. And if you don't have a fish poacher, use a roasting pan and cover it securely with foil.

- 2 cups dry white wine
  Juice of 1 large lemon
- 2¼ cups scraped and thinly sliced carrots
- 1¾ cups thinly sliced celery
- 2 medium onions, coarsely chopped
- 3 bay leaves
- 4 quarts cold water
- 6 pounds whole fish, cleaned, with head and tail on

GARNISH
- 1 *each* red and yellow bell pepper, roasted, cleaned, and cut into strips
  Lettuce leaves
- 4 hard-cooked eggs
- 2 bunches green onions, trimmed
- 3 lemons, cut into wedges

Place all ingredients except fish and garnish into a fish poacher. Bring to a boil and simmer for 30 minutes. Wrap the fish well in several thicknesses of

cheesecloth and carefully lower it into the court-bouillon. Cover and barely simmer for 20 minutes, or until flesh is firm and white. Cool in the liquid and chill (still in the liquid).

To serve, drain fish, pat dry, and carefully scrape off the skin. You may also remove and discard the head and tail if you choose. Garnish with roasted red and yellow pepper strips, lettuce, hard-cooked eggs cut into eighths, green onions, and lemon wedges.

Serve with Fresh Cucumber Sauce (recipe follows).

Serves 6 to 8

FRESH CUCUMBER SAUCE

- 1 **cup low-fat sour cream**
- 1 **teaspoon salt**
- 1 **teaspoon Dijon-style mustard**
- 2 **teaspoons red wine vinegar**
- 2 **tablespoons coarsely chopped sweet pickle**
- 1 **teaspoon sweet pickle juice**
- 2 **medium cucumbers, peeled, seeded, and diced small**
  Paprika to taste (optional)

Whisk together all the ingredients except the cucumber and paprika. Just before serving, drain and dry the cucumber and fold it into the sauce. Sprinkle the top with paprika if you like.

Makes about 2 cups

RICE, GREEN PEA, AND OLIVE SALAD WITH ORANGE-CILANTRO VINAIGRETTE

I use frozen tiny green peas in this salad, uncooked but thawed at the last minute. And I cook the rice in chicken stock.

- 3 **cups cooked rice**
- ⅔ **cup sliced pitted green olives**
- 1 **cup frozen tiny green peas**
- 3 **tablespoons olive oil**
- 6 **tablespoons fresh orange juice**
- 1 **tablespoon grated orange rind**
- 1 **tablespoon fresh lemon rind**
- 1 **teaspoon salt, or to taste**
- ½ **teaspoon paprika**
- ¼ **cup finely chopped cilantro**

Toss rice and olives together. Place peas in a strainer and let very hot tap water run over them for a minute, shaking, to thaw. Shake dry and add to the rice and olives. Toss.

Whisk together all the other ingredients and dress the salad just before serving, tossing well.

Serves 6 to 8

COCONUT FLAN

This recipe uses lots of coconut, which gives it plenty of flavor and crunch. It's delicious as is — or serve it with fruit.

- 1½ **cups sugar**
- ½ **cup cold water**
  Pinch of cream of tartar
- 4 **large eggs, separated**
- 2 **cups coconut water (add milk to this if you don't have enough from the coconut)**
- 1 **4-ounce can sweetened condensed milk**
- 1 **teaspoon coconut extract**
- 1 **teaspoon vanilla extract**
- 2 **cups grated coconut**

Combine sugar, water, and cream of tartar in a small skillet. Boil over medium-high heat without stirring until

ABOVE: *Coconut Flan.* OPPOSITE: *Cold Poached Gulf Fish with Fresh Cucumber Sauce and the Rice, Green Pea, and Olive Salad.*

sugar is melted, about 3 to 4 minutes. Swirl mixture once as it begins to caramelize in about 5 minutes. Turn heat back slightly and continue cooking until mixture turns a deep golden color, swirling occasionally, about another 10 to 12 minutes. Pour into a 6-cup loaf pan. Using a hot pad, tilt the pan back and forth to coat the inside as the caramel cools and thickens.

Preheat the oven to 350 degrees and put a kettle of water on to heat.

Combine egg yolks, coconut water, condensed milk, coconut extract, and vanilla. Mix well, then fold in the grated coconut. Whip egg whites until just frothy and combine with other ingredients. Pour into prepared pan. Place the pan in a larger pan and surround with hot water. Bake until golden on top and a knife inserted in the center comes out clean, about 1 hour and 5 or 10 minutes.

Cool and refrigerate. To serve, run a knife around the edges and unmold onto a deep platter, being careful not to spill the caramel that accumulates in the bottom of the baking pan.

Serves 6 to 8

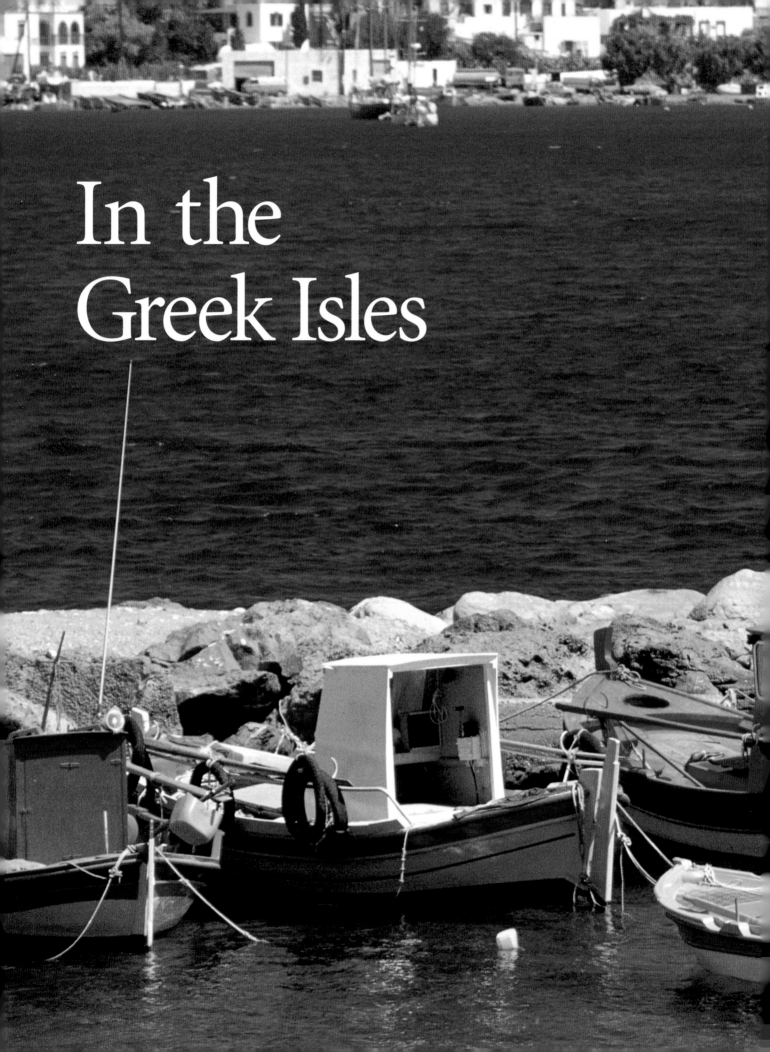

In the
Greek Isles

 NE OF THE WONDERFUL things about the magical Greek island of Patmos is that its very limitations make me try harder. This dry, rocky spot of land, some ten hours distant by ferry from the mainland, is not very hospitable to tender growing things. Even the surrounding Aegean is stingy with its bounty, so the raw material for a meal is anything but varied. What's available is an odd assortment: eggplant, squid and one or two other types of fish, rice and pasta, tomatoes, cucumbers, black olives, a few mild cheeses, yogurt, olive oil, garlic, mint, eggs, and frozen meats — with fruit imported from the other islands and even farther afield. Occasionally a surprise will turn up once in the market, never to be seen again after the original shipment is finished. How many combinations can you make from that? Well, let's see. Improvising is part of the fun.

And of course, when friends arrive for a visit they always bring along some simple treat, such as balsamic vinegar (or yesterday's *New York Times*). The funny thing about this stuff — so taken for granted at home and which a house guest would almost certainly feel was inappropriate under other circumstances — is that it assumes such great importance here.

After a few weeks without the largess of the local supermarket and newsstand, you start to yearn for the damnedest things — a peanut butter and jelly sandwich (which you seldom, if ever, eat at home), or perhaps even, gulp, *New York* magazine.

But back to the puzzle at hand. It always fascinates me how the food of one place can have its comfortable equivalent in another. For instance, our Louisiana cook used to make pecan-coated

ABOVE: *Coming from the market.*
OPPOSITE: *View across the island.*

fish, which everyone loved. On Patmos, there wasn't a pecan in sight, but pistachios were plentiful on the island. At home the fish was served with a typical tartar sauce, but here the sauce is that classic cucumber, garlic, and yogurt mixture called *tzatjiki*. I almost hate to admit it, but I'm beginning to think I like my Greek version better than the Southern one. The spell of the islands at work no doubt.

Whatever, it's part of the fun to see what you can create from local ingredients. Of course, there are times when this sure makes you appreciate what you don't have. Character building, I hope.

Under the Arbor

L AMB IS ONE of the only meats you can regularly buy fresh in the market on Patmos, so we made it the center of a menu, to be served with rice. After that was a surprise salad and finally a delicious tart. Incidentally, the bread on the island isn't really terrific, so we sliced it thin and made melba toast from it by leaving it in a 250-degree oven for about 45 minutes. A vast improvement.

OUZO LEMON LAMB WITH YOGURT

BUTTERED RICE

MELBA TOAST AND SWEET BUTTER

PEACH, TOMATO, BEET, AND RED ONION SALAD
WITH GRAPEFRUIT VINAIGRETTE

HONEY NUT TART

OPPOSITE TOP: *Ouzo Lemon Lamb with Yogurt and Buttered Rice.* ABOVE: *Under the arbor.* LEFT: *An outdoor settee.*

OUZO LEMON LAMB WITH YOGURT

The lemon zest in this dish gives it a nice zing and the cayenne a bit of bite. A good combo.

- 3 pounds boneless lamb, cut from the leg

MARINADE
- ½ cup ouzo
- 1 cup beef stock
- 2 medium garlic cloves, crushed
- 1 small onion, coarsely chopped
- 6-inch sprig rosemary, leaves stripped off, or 1 tablespoon dried
- 2 medium bay leaves, broken into several pieces
- 2 dozen fresh mint leaves, coarsely chopped
- 3 tablespoons fresh lemon juice
- 1 teaspoon salt
- 1 teaspoon black pepper

TO COMPLETE THE DISH
- ¾ teaspoon salt
- ¾ teaspoon black pepper
- 2 tablespoons olive oil
- 2 tablespoons unsalted butter
- 2 cups chopped onions
- 2 tablespoons flour
- 2 cups beef broth
- 3 generous tablespoons coarsely chopped lemon zest
- Generous pinch of cayenne pepper
- 1 teaspoon paprika
- 1 cup plain yogurt
- Lemon zest strips for garnish (optional)
- Mint sprigs for garnish (optional)

Marinate the lamb: Cut the lamb into 2-inch cubes. Carefully trim off all gristle, fat, and connective tissue. You should wind up with about 2½ pounds of trimmed lamb. Set aside.

Combine all the ingredients for the marinade in a large glass or ceramic bowl and whisk together. Add lamb, tossing lightly and pressing down gently so that it is completely covered with the liquid. Cover tightly and marinate overnight in the refrigerator.

Complete the dish: Remove the lamb from the marinade and pat dry. Discard marinade, then generously salt and pepper the lamb. Set aside.

In a large, heavy skillet, heat the oil and butter together over high heat. When very hot, quickly brown meat on all sides, placing it in a large pot as it is finished. When all meat is browned, add the chopped onions and sauté, over medium-high heat, until wilted and beginning to brown, about 2 minutes. Sprinkle with flour and mix. Continue to cook, moving mixture around with a spatula, until flour turns golden, another 3 minutes. Scrape the mixture into the pot with the lamb. Deglaze skillet with the beef broth and add to the pot. Bring to a simmer and add lemon zest, cayenne, and, if necessary, salt and pepper to taste. Simmmer until lamb is tender, about 15 minutes. Stir in paprika and yogurt and serve over a bed of rice. Garnish with lemon zest strips and sprigs of mint.
Serves 6

ABOVE: *Island donkeys.* OPPOSITE: *Bell tower of one of the local churches.*

PEACH, TOMATO, BEET, AND RED ONION SALAD WITH GRAPEFRUIT VINAIGRETTE

One morning, to our delight, all the markets had fresh beets and grapefruit, so we prepared this salad — which is one I make whenever I can get fresh beets.

6 small or 4 medium-to-large fresh beets
1 large grapefruit
¼ cup olive oil
1 teaspoon mild yellow mustard
1 teaspoon salt
¼ teaspoon black pepper
1 teaspoon light vinegar
¼ teaspoon Worcestershire sauce
½ teaspoon honey
6 small or 4 medium peaches, skinned, pitted, and cut into thick slices
6 small or 4 medium tomatoes, skinned and cut into eighths
1 small red onion, cut into thin rings

Preheat the oven to 400 degrees.

Line a small pan with foil. Cut off beet tops, leaving about ½ inch of stem. Do not cut off root. Wash and place in the lined pan. Cover securely with foil. Bake until tender, about 1 hour. Allow to cool slightly; cut off tops and skins will slip off. Rub with a little vegetable oil to keep from drying out and set aside.

Peel off grapefruit rind and, over a small bowl, divide into sections; slit each section open and remove skin and pith, letting the pulp and juice drop into the bowl. This will be broken into small chunks.

Whisk together the oil, mustard, salt, pepper, vinegar, Worcestershire sauce, and honey. Mix in with the grapefruit pulp and juice. Set aside.

To serve, cut beets into eighths and place in a bowl with the peaches, tomatoes, and onion. Lightly toss. Stir vinaigrette and spoon enough over the vegetables and fruit to coat well. Serve extra vinaigrette on the side.

You may make a composed salad of this by arranging the peaches, tomatoes, and beets on a plate and topping with the onion rings. Spoon vinaigrette over each.
Serves 6

———

BUTTERED RICE

For more flavor, cook the rice in beef stock. But for this particular dish, I don't think it is necessary.

2 cups long-grain rice
  Salt to taste
1 tablespoon unsalted butter
1 tablespoon olive oil

Place rice in a medium saucepan and cover with 3 inches of well-salted water. Bring to a boil over high heat. After it has boiled, uncovered, for 9 minutes, test for doneness. If not quite tender, boil it for another minute or so until done. Pour into a colander and wash well with hot water. Rinse out saucepan and add butter and oil. Heat and add rice, tossing to coat.
Makes about 4 cups

OPPOSITE: *Peach, Tomato, Beet, and Red Onion Salad.* ABOVE: *Bougainvillea and more bougainvillea.* BELOW: *View of a church on a terraced hillside.*

HONEY NUT TART

I was very pleased to see the great variety of shelled nuts available. Perfect for a tart. We mixed them all up.

If the tart in the picture looks large, that's because it is. We had all the ingredients, but not the tart pan, so we improvised with a large ovenproof (luckily) tray.

By the way, when we made the pastry for this tart, we made an extra half-recipe to use for the sugar sticks to go with the sorbet on page 54.

PASTRY

- 1 **cup all-purpose flour**
- 2 **tablespoons sugar**
  Pinch of salt
- ½ **cup (1 stick) unsalted butter, cut into bits and frozen**
- 3 **tablespoons ice water**

FILLING

- 3 **large eggs, lightly beaten**
- ½ **cup sugar**
- ½ **cup honey**
- 2 **cups mixed toasted nuts (almonds, walnuts, and hazelnuts)**
- 1½ **teaspoons lemon juice**
- 1 **teaspoon vanilla extract**

  Plain yogurt with honey for serving

Make the pastry: Place the flour, sugar, salt, and frozen butter in a food processor. Process until butter is the size of large peas. Add ice water and process until mixture can be gathered into a ball. Place between 2 sheets of waxed paper and flatten slightly. Refrigerate or freeze until ready to use.

Finish the tart: Preheat the oven to 375 degrees. Line a 9-inch tart pan with the rolled-out pastry and set aside.

Mix the eggs, sugar, and honey. Stir in the nuts, lemon juice, and vanilla. Pour into prepared shell and bake until slightly puffy and a knife comes out clean, about 50 to 60 minutes.

Serve topped with yogurt and a drizzle of honey.

Serves 6 to 8

OPPOSITE: *Honey Nut Tart.* TOP: *Bell tower.* ABOVE: *Mosaic floor.* OVERLEAF: *View of the monastery.*

ABOVE: *Papa Gouras's Lemon Chicken, Shredded Zucchini, and Lentils with Cucumber.* RIGHT: *Plumbago.* OPPOSITE TOP: *A secluded shore.* OPPOSITE BOTTOM: *Table set for lunch.*

Overlooking the Aegean

PAPA GOURAS, of Patmian House — a restaurant only a few minutes' walk from our house — taught us to make the delicious chicken in this menu. I have a feeling it will continue to make appearances now that I'm back home.

FRESH TOMATO AND FETA CHEESE ASPIC WITH MAYONNAISE

PAPA GOURAS'S LEMON CHICKEN

LENTILS WITH CUCUMBER

SHREDDED ZUCCHINI

APPLE SORBET WITH SUGAR STICKS

FRESH TOMATO AND FETA CHEESE ASPIC WITH MAYONNAISE

Shades of my childhood, when we used to have tomato aspic at least several times a week. Of course, without feta.

> 5 tablespoons water
> 2 tablespoons unflavored gelatin
> 4 cups tomato pulp (see *Note*)
> 1½ teaspoons salt
> 1 medium green bell pepper
> 1 small onion
> 2 tablespoons lemon juice
> 1 tablespoon Worcestershire sauce
> ½ teaspoon Tabasco
> 1 cup feta cheese, in ¼-inch cubes

Put water in a deep saucer and sprinkle gelatin over it. Set aside.

Place tomato pulp in a small saucepan and stir in salt. Grate the green pepper and onion over the tomato pulp, allowing the juice and pulp of the pepper and onion to drop into the pan. Stir in lemon juice, Worcestershire sauce, and Tabasco.

Heat mixture over medium heat and stir in softened gelatin. Continue to heat and stir until gelatin is dissolved, just a minute.

Pour half the mixture into a 4- to 6-cup ring mold. Place in the refrigerator. Allow the balance of the tomato mixture to cool in the saucepan for about 30 minutes, then put it in the refrigerator. When the mixture in the mold is beginning to set — in about an hour or so — sprinkle the cheese over it and carefully pour the second batch of tomato mixture over the cheese. Some cheese may float to the top; if so, press it below the surface gently with your fingers or the back of a spoon. Return to the refrigerator and allow to jell completely, another hour at least.

An hour before serving, unmold by placing the mold in a pan of hot water just long enough to loosen the aspic, about 30 seconds. Place the serving plate over the mold and quickly invert. If the aspic does not come out, hold the inverted mold tightly against the plate and give it a good downward shake or two to loosen it. Return unmolded aspic to the refrigerator for an hour to allow any melted aspic to set again.

Serve with Homemade Mayonnaise (page 34).
Serves 6 to 8

Note: There are several ways of "making" the tomato pulp, and my favorite is to roast the tomatoes. To do this, you place about a dozen ripe medium tomatoes on a pan and put them under the broiler. Let them blacken, as you do red bell peppers, turning as the skin darkens and burns. Remove tomatoes to a plate and allow them to sit until cool, about an hour. They will give up a great deal of water, which you throw away. Cut out the stem end and discard the skin. Put tomatoes through a strainer to remove seeds. Twelve tomatoes should give you about 4 cups of pulp, but this is rather inexact. If you are a little short, add tomato juice.

We didn't have a broiler here, so I cut the tomatoes into large chunks and cooked them over medium-low heat until they were soft, about 30 minutes. Then I pureed them and strained out the seeds and skin.

PAPA GOURAS'S LEMON CHICKEN

Here it is — as promised.

- 1 cup dry white wine
- 1 cup beef stock
- 3 generous tablespoons minced shallots
- 3 tablespoons lemon juice
- ½ teaspoon salt
- ½ cup (1 stick) unsalted butter, softened, plus 2 tablespoons
- 3 teaspoons grated lemon zest
- 6 5- to 6-ounce boned chicken breasts, slightly flattened
  Flour
- 2 large eggs, lightly beaten
- 2 tablespoons olive oil

Place the wine, stock, shallots, and lemon juice in a small pot and reduce to about ¼ cup over high heat, about 25 minutes. Stir in salt and allow to cool. When slightly warmer than room temperature, whisk in the softened ½ cup butter, a few tablespoons at a time, until mixture is the consistency of mayonnaise. Beat in lemon zest and set this lemon butter aside.

Dredge the flattened chicken breasts in flour, shaking off excess, then place in the beaten egg, allowing excess to drain off, then once more in flour. Shake off any excess. Place aside carefully. Put the remaining 2 tablespoons of butter and the olive oil in a large heavy skillet. Over medium-high heat, sauté the chicken breasts until golden on both sides, about 5 minutes in total. Transfer to a warm plate and spread some of the lemon butter over the top of each.
Serves 6

Note: The amount of lemon butter in this recipe makes enough for 12 or more servings of chicken. Any leftover may be refrigerated, covered. Allow to return to room temperature before using again.

LENTILS WITH CUCUMBER

This could easily be made into a soup by adding more chicken stock and letting minced cucumber be a garnish.

- 2 tablespoons olive oil
- 1 cup chopped onion
- 1¼ cups dried brown lentils
- 4 cups strong chicken stock, heated
- 1 teaspoon red wine vinegar
- ¼ teaspoon black pepper
  Salt to taste
- 6 tablespoons, peeled, seeded, and chopped cucumber

Place 1 tablespoon of the olive oil in a medium saucepan and sauté the onions over medium-high heat until turning brown, about 5 minutes. Add lentils and hot stock. Bring back to a medium-low boil and boil uncovered until tender, about 50 to 60 minutes, stirring occasionally toward the end of the cooking time. Add more stock if lentils are getting too dry, but most of the liquid should be boiled down by the time the lentils are tender. Stir in the remaining tablespoon of olive oil, vinegar, black pepper, and salt. Toss with cucumbers.
Serves 6 to 8

SHREDDED ZUCCHINI

Not only is this fast, but it is also my favorite way of preparing zucchini.

- 2 cups shredded zucchini
- 1 teaspoon salt
- 2 generous tablespoons unsalted butter
- ½ cup coarsely chopped onion

Place the shredded zucchini in a colander, sprinkle with the salt, and toss. Put in the sink or over a plate and cover with a tea towel. Allow to drain for at least 1 hour. Discard the accumulated liquid from the plate and squeeze as much additional liquid from the zucchini as possible. Set aside.

Melt the butter in a large skillet over medium heat and add the onion. Sauté until wilted and lightly browned, about 5 minutes. Add the zucchini and toss. Continue to cook over medium heat until zucchini is turning tender, about 6 to 8 minutes. Do not overcook.
Serves 6

OPPOSITE: *Fresh Tomato and Feta Cheese Aspic with Mayonnaise.* BELOW: *Interior of a Patmos house.*

APPLE SORBET WITH SUGAR STICKS

Our market got in a shipment of rather sad-looking apples. But since everyone was getting a little tired of peaches, as marvelous as they had been, and since our house came equipped with an ice-cream machine, we decided to buy some and make sorbet.

- 4 **small tart apples, peeled, cored, and quartered**
- ⅔ **cup sugar**
- 2 **teaspoons lemon juice**
- 1 **cup water**
  Calvados or other apple brandy (optional)
  Sugar Sticks (recipe follows)

Place the apples, sugar, lemon juice, and water in a medium saucepan and simmer until apples are tender, about 10 minutes. Puree and allow to cool.

Freeze in an ice-cream freezer according to the manufacturer's directions. When serving, you may make an indentation in the top of each serving with the back of a spoon and fill with brandy, preferably Calvados.
Makes approximately 1 quart

SUGAR STICKS

These are great with any kind of sorbet or ice cream. They are best made with the kind of coarse granulated sugar you see in the photograph.

- ½ **recipe Nut Tart Pastry (see page 47)**
- 1 **cup coarse sugar**

Refrigerate the pastry dough for at least 6 hours before using.

Preheat the oven to 350 degrees.

Roll out the dough on waxed paper to about ¼ inch thick. Sprinkle another sheet of paper with about half the sugar and invert rolled-out dough, which is very sticky, onto it and peel off top paper. Sprinkle with more sugar. Cut into ½-inch strips and cut each into a stick about 5 or 6 inches long. Place on a cookie sheet and bake until turning golden and bottoms have caramelized, about 15 to 20 minutes. Do not burn bottoms.

Meanwhile, sprinkle another sheet of waxed paper with more sugar. After sticks have cooled about a minute, quickly remove each and place it, bottom side up, onto the sugared paper. If sticks stay too long in the pan after baking, they will stick, so lift them off as soon as they can be handled without breaking.

Allow to cool and store in an airtight container.
Makes about 2 dozen

ABOVE: *Vine-capped doorway.*
OPPOSITE: *Apple Sorbet with Sugar Sticks.*

LEFT: *Patmian landscape.* TOP: *Painted chest.* ABOVE: *Terrace planters.*

Early Dinner

THE DINING ROOM of our house looked out onto a terrace below and into olive trees farther away. It was furnished with not only a dining table and cabinets for holding the dinnerware, silver, and linen but with those ubiquitous Greek backless sofas, which were arranged to create a little seating space for having coffee after dinner. There were windows on adjacent walls but they were on the opposite side of the room from where the dining table stood.

The afternoon light was so glorious streaming through these windows that we would often move the table over for our early dinners so it could be bathed in golden light and we could look out at the trees and flowers. What serenity.

**PISTACHIO-COATED FISH
WITH CUCUMBER SAUCE**

**ORZO WITH ONIONS AND
BLACK OLIVES**

BAKED HONEY-MINT TOMATOES

**PEACH BREAD PUDDING WITH
BRANDY JAM SAUCE**

TOP: *Flowers outside the house.* ABOVE: *View into the bedroom.* RIGHT: *Patmian door.* OPPOSITE: *Table set for dinner.*

PISTACHIO-COATED FISH

Here is my Greek version of Louisiana nut-coated fish.

6 ½-inch-thick milk-white fish filets, about 1¾ pounds
   Milk
   Salt and black pepper to taste
   Flour
1 large egg, beaten with 3 to 4 tablespoons milk
1 cup fresh soft bread crumbs
1 cup coarsely ground pistachio nuts
3 tablespoons unsalted butter
1 tablespoon vegetable oil
   Cucumber Sauce (recipe follows)
   Lemon wedges

Place fish in a shallow bowl and cover with milk. Refrigerate, covered, for several hours.

Drain off milk and pat filets dry. Salt and pepper on all sides and set aside.

Set up a little assembly line. Put about a cup of flour onto a sheet of waxed paper, beside that a low bowl holding the beaten egg, and finally another sheet of waxed paper with the bread crumbs and nuts tossed together. Next to these have another sheet of waxed paper or a platter to hold the coated filets.

Dredge each filet in flour, shaking off excess. Next dip it into the egg mixture, letting excess drain off, and then put it into the nut mixture, coating it well by pressing it lightly. Carefully transfer to the platter.

Heat half the butter and oil in a large skillet over medium heat. When hot, slide in the first 3 filets and brown on both sides, cooking until done, about 3 to 4 minutes in total. It is best not to turn these more than once so as not to break off the crust. Add the remaining butter and oil and quickly cook the other 3 filets, while keeping the first batch warm in a low oven.

Serve immediately with the sauce and lemon wedges.

Serves 6

CUCUMBER SAUCE

There are as many versions of this sauce, called *tzatjiki* in Greece, as there are recipes for mayonnaise in France. All the differences are small, but each person swears by his or her own. One important thing to remember is that the yogurt is milder in Greece and that the garlic is, too. So maybe a combination of garlic and shallots would be a good idea for making it at home in the U. S.

1 medium cucumber, peeled, seeded, and chopped fine
1 cup plain yogurt
1 tablespoon olive oil
1 tablespoon lemon juice
¼ teaspoon salt
1 large garlic clove, minced
1 tablespoon chopped fresh dill (optional)

Combine all ingredients, cover, and refrigerate for at least an hour to let flavor develop.

Makes about 1½ cups

ORZO WITH ONIONS AND BLACK OLIVES

Orzo with onions and olives is always a winner. I serve it very often in both summer and winter.

- 4 tablespoons (½ stick) unsalted butter
- 2 cups coarsely chopped onions
- 1 generous cup pitted and drained oil-cured black olives
- 2 cups orzo
  Salt and black pepper to taste

Melt the butter over medium to low heat and add the onions. Sauté until soft but not browned, about 5 minutes. Toss in the olives and set aside.

To assemble the dish, boil the orzo in well-salted water until tender, about 9 to 10 minutes, and drain well. Place onion-olive mixture over low heat to warm it, then toss orzo in with it. Salt and pepper to taste.
Serves 6 to 8

BAKED HONEY-MINT TOMATOES

If this has a familiar ring to it, you are right. Baked honey tomatoes is a Southern dish and a version of it made an appearance with its Southern cousin in my book *Southern Food & Plantation Houses*. Shows you how adaptable foods of one region are to another. They had never seen it here on Patmos.

- 6 medium tomatoes
- 6 tablespoons fresh coarse bread crumbs
- 1½ teaspoons salt
- 1½ teaspoons black pepper
- 2 tablespoons finely minced fresh mint
- 1 tablespoon honey
  Few drops Tabasco (optional)
- 1 tablespoon unsalted butter

Preheat the oven to 350 degrees.

Slice off the stem ends of the tomatoes and carefully scoop out the seeds. Place open side up in a buttered baking dish. Mix the bread crumbs with the salt, pepper, and mint. Drizzle honey over the tomatoes, rubbing it down into the cavities. (You may mix a few drops of Tabasco with the honey if you like.) Sprinkle with the crumbs and dot with butter. Bake, uncovered, for 30 minutes, until skins begin to wrinkle. Place under broiler for another 5 minutes, or until crumbs begin to brown.

Serve hot or at room temperature.
Serves 6

PEACH BREAD PUDDING WITH BRANDY JAM SAUCE

The Patmian bread was perfect for this dish. I cut it the night before and left it uncovered to go stale overnight.

- 12 ½-inch-thick slices stale French or white Italian bread, trimmed into regular rectangles
- 6 tablespoons unsalted butter, softened
- 8 small peaches, skinned, pitted, and thickly sliced
- 3 large eggs
- ½ cup honey
- 2 cups milk
- ¼ teaspoon grated nutmeg
- 1 teaspoon vanilla extract
- 1 or more tablespoons sugar

Preheat the oven to 350 degrees and put a kettle of water on to heat.

Select a low-sided 6-cup baking dish and place the bread slices in the bottom, cutting them so they will cover the entire surface. (You will need more or less than the 12 slices.) Remove bread and set aside. Generously butter the dish and cover its bottom with the peach slices. Generously butter (use it all) the cut bread slices and place them on top of the peaches. With a fork, beat the eggs and honey together. Pour this into the milk and mix well. Stir in the nutmeg and vanilla. Carefully strain the milk mixture into the dish. The buttered bread will float up. Sprinkle the buttered tops of the bread well with the sugar. Place dish in a larger pan, put in the oven, and surround with hot water. Bake until bread starts turning golden and a knife comes out clean when it is inserted, 40 to 45 minutes. You may run pudding under the broiler to brown the bread a bit more and melt the sugar.

Serve at room temperature or chilled with Brandy Jam Sauce (recipe follows).
Serves 6 to 8

BRANDY JAM SAUCE

- ½ cup jam (we used peach)
- ¼ cup water
- 2 tablespoons lemon juice
- ¼ cup brandy

Combine jam and water in a small saucepan. Bring to a boil over medium heat, stirring to reduce slightly, about a minute. Off the heat stir in the lemon juice and brandy. Allow to cool.
Makes about ¾ cup

OPPOSITE: *Pistachio-Coated Fish, Cucumber Sauce, Orzo with Onions and Black Olives, and Baked Honey-Mint Tomatoes.* LEFT: *Peach Bread Pudding.*

Patmian Breakfast

I'VE GOT TO BE HONEST — yogurt is not my favorite thing. I eat it and cook with it, but never crave it. The same is true to a lesser degree of honey. But both these things are so flavorful on Patmos I have almost become a convert. I should note, though, that Greek yogurt is creamier and does not have the bite our American product has. It is in some ways more like crème fraîche. In fact, you can approximate its taste by combining crème fraîche with plain yogurt in equal amounts.

One morning in the market we came across a box of small Macedonian peaches that were truly scrumptious; combined with the local yogurt and honey, they made the centerpiece of a wonderful breakfast.

Of course, this breakfast would be good any place, so try it at home. The Graviera cheese has a texture and taste similar to Gruyère, which could be substituted.

The peach, yogurt, and honey combination would also make a fine summer dessert.

PEACHES WITH YOGURT AND HONEY

DRY TOAST

GRAVIERA CHEESE

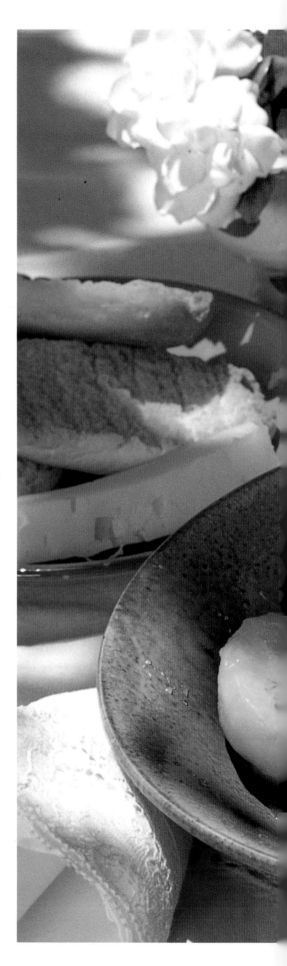

ABOVE: *Ancient stone arches.* RIGHT: *Patmian breakfast.*

In Tuscany

IN THE VILLAGES and hilly environs of Tuscany there is a stillness at midday and early afternoon that is almost tangible. Whenever I think of the place, it's this singular characteristic that almost invariably comes to mind. It's no wonder that this part of the world has become so popular a summer vacation choice for overstimulated city types.

To get there you have to either drive or take a train, since planes bring you only part of the way. And it is this last leg of the journey — in early summer through fields of sunflowers that roll away into the valley; past hills, their upper ridges lined by slim silhouetted cypresses pointed devoutly heavenward and crowned by medieval fortress towns — that plunges you into Tuscany's spell. The spell continues as you settle down.

Our house was a typical eighteenth-century stone structure with a tile roof that once sheltered a family with a thriving farm. It has a covered outdoor spot for dining and an arbor out back. Like all the neighboring buildings, it seems to magically nestle into its surroundings.

In this land where the mysterious Etruscans once flourished, and where the Renaissance flowered, I soon fall into a routine that allows me to balance work and ease. But at the beginning we seem to do little more than talk about what we are *going* to do — a sure sign that we're on the right track. It usually takes the imminent arrival of house guests or overnight visitors to get us really organized. Soon our days begin to alternate between working mornings and sightseeing mornings. There are more places of historic (and artistic) interest within an hour or so's drive, no matter where you are in Tuscany,

ABOVE: *Tuscan thistles.* OPPOSITE: *Sheep herder.*

than you could exhaust in a dozen visits. Some of these I've visited before, and I love returning with friends to share in the pleasure I know they'll have. One such place is a meticulously maintained abbey called Monte Oliveto Maggiore. Should you ever find yourself in Tuscany, don't fail to make time to visit there. Being slightly off the beaten track, it's never crowded and it is today, if anything, more glorious than it was in the fifteenth century when the surrounding forest of black cypress was first planted.

Anyway, on our excursion days we usually lunch at a restaurant. Consequently, our evening meals tend toward the light and unstructured. Even on at-home days our eating habits seem to be more erratic here. Lunches are combinations of the sort of easy concoctions that may be put together with a minimum of effort — and which may be added to to become part of a later meal. Of course, once or twice a week we get in the mood and cook up a storm. This free-form attitude must obviously somehow reflect the Tuscan tradition of forthright simplicity in such matters as cooking and dining. Whatever, it suits us.

Four Pastas

IT'S INTERESTING that many serious food people you meet hereabout will ultimately get around to telling you that pasta is not truly Tuscan. This small conceit is strangely at odds with reality, since pasta in one form or another is on every menu in every restaurant you visit. And rumor has it that it's been a mainstay of the Italian diet ever since Marco Polo had the wit to see the possibilities of the stuff and bring it back to Venice from China, among the bales of silk and barrels of spices.

Heedless of our lack of Tuscan purity, we serve pasta often and simply, with either a plate of tomatoes before or a green salad after. When we want a dessert, generally there's poached fruit in the refrigerator (see page 78) with something like shortbread (see page 76) to dip into the poaching liquid.

Incidentally, you'll probably notice that the pasta portions are fairly modest. I've come to realize that for meals made of several courses, serving the typical big plate of pasta means that by the time you get to the salad and dessert you are almost too sated to appreciate it. Balance is everything!

Among the wines we particularly like are a crisp white, Le Grance, and the well-known Brunello, a full-bodied red. Of course, we tasted lots of others, but we seem always to come back to these two.

OPPOSITE: *In the market.*
BELOW: *A local crest.*

ABOVE: *Spaghetti with Garlic and Rosemary Oil.* BELOW: *Rigatoni with White Beans, Green Beans, and Pine Nuts.*

ABOVE: *Fettuccini with Red Bell Pepper Sauce.* BELOW: *Bucatini with Black Pepper, Bread Crumbs, and Pecorino.*

FETTUCCINI WITH RED BELL PEPPER SAUCE

This is the same sauce we serve with our stuffed crepes (page 92). It may be used in many other ways — on fish or slices of roast veal.

- 2 tablespoons unsalted butter
- 2 tablespoons olive oil
- 2¼ cups chopped red onions
- 2 large garlic cloves, minced
- 3 large red bell peppers, roasted, peeled, seeded, and chopped
- 2 cups chicken stock
- ¼ teaspoon black pepper
  Salt to taste
- ¾ pound fettuccini
  Grated Parmesan cheese to taste

Place the butter and oil in a large skillet over medium heat and sauté onions until they start to turn slightly brown in spots, about 4 minutes. Add the garlic and sauté another minute. Add the peppers and cook another 2 minutes. Add stock and black pepper. Cook for 10 minutes. Transfer to a food processor and puree. Salt to taste.

Cook the pasta in salted water according to directions on the box. Toss with sauce and place in heated individual bowls. Serve with grated Parmesan.
Serves 6

———

SPAGHETTI WITH GARLIC AND ROSEMARY OIL

This flavored oil was inspired by something I read by the great Marcella Hazan. If you have time, make this sauce the day before and leave it out in a cool spot, unrefrigerated and unstrained.

The oil is also delicious brushed on bread and grilled.

- 2 tablespoons olive oil
- 6 tablespoons unsalted butter
- 4 3-inch pieces fresh rosemary
- 4 large garlic cloves, coarsely chopped

- 1 cup beef broth reduced to 1 tablespoon, about 20 minutes
- ¾ pound spaghetti
  Grated Parmesan cheese to taste

Heat the olive oil and butter over medium heat in a small pot. Add the rosemary and garlic. Cook until the garlic begins to soften and brown lightly, about 5 minutes. Stir in the reduced broth and set aside.

Cook the pasta until *al dente* in salted water according to directions on the box. Strain the infused oil over it. Toss. Serve with Parmesan cheese on the side.
Serves 6

———

RIGATONI WITH WHITE BEANS, GREEN BEANS, AND PINE NUTS

The combination of white and green beans, with or without pine nuts, dressed simply with olive oil makes a fine side dish with any meat.

- 1 cup dried cannellini beans, soaked overnight
- 6 cups flavorful chicken stock
- 1 teaspoon dried oregano
  Pinch of cayenne pepper
- 2 large garlic cloves, crushed
- 1½ cups tipped, stemmed, and snapped green beans
  Generous ¾ cup toasted pine nuts
- ¼ cup olive oil
- 4 tablespoons (½ stick) unsalted butter
  Salt and black pepper to taste
- ¾ pound rigatoni
  Grated Parmesan cheese to taste

Drain the soaked cannellini beans and cover with 4 cups of the stock. Add the oregano, cayenne, and garlic. Bring to a medium boil, then reduce heat to low. Simmer until very tender, about 1 hour and 10 minutes. Cool in the liquid.

Cover the green beans with the balance of the stock and bring to a

simmer over medium heat. Cook until just beginning to get tender, about 9 minutes. Set the beans aside to cool in the liquid.

To serve, cook rigatoni in salted water until tender, according to the directions on the box. Meanwhile, in a skillet heat 2 tablespoons each of the oil and butter. Drain the cannellini and green beans, add to the skillet, and heat in the oil and butter. Place balance of the oil and butter in a large bowl and heat it in the oven. Drain the pasta and put into the heated bowl, then toss to coat. Add cannellini and green beans

Tuscan hill town.

and toss. Place in individual heated bowls and sprinkle with pine nuts. Serve with grated Parmesan cheese.
Serves 6

BUCATINI WITH BLACK PEPPER, BREAD CRUMBS, AND PECORINO

The bread crumbs give this a little extra crunch, but leave them out if you're in a hurry; Parmesan could be substituted for the pecorino. Incidentally, bucatini is very large spaghetti.

¼ cup olive oil

4 tablespoons (½ stick) unsalted butter

1 cup grated hard pecorino cheese

1 tablespoon black pepper, or to taste

¾ pound bucatini

1 cup toasted fresh bread crumbs

Heat the oil and butter together. Combine the cheese and pepper. Cook the pasta until tender in salted water, drain, and put into a heated bowl. Pour the oil and butter over and toss quickly.

Add the cheese and pepper and toss again. Place in individual serving bowls and top each serving with a sprinkling of bread crumbs.
Serves 6

Two Fennel Salads

IN MY MIND fennel is almost synonymous with Italy. As a matter of fact, I never ate it much until I started having it in Italian restaurants. It makes a wonderful salad but is also terrific as an appetizer, braised in a little chicken stock, topped with shaved Parmesan, and run under the broiler.

Fennel also becomes a good side dish when baked or simmered in stock and then pureed with just a little cooked rice to give it body.

FENNEL AND ORANGE SALAD WITH SHAVED PARMESAN AND BLACK OLIVES

You may substitute peaches for the oranges in this salad.

- 6 medium to small seedless oranges, peeled with pith scraped
- 6 small or 3 medium fennel bulbs, trimmed and cored
- 36 black olives in oil
- 2 tablespoons balsamic vinegar
- 1 teaspoon Dijon-style mustard
- ¾ teaspoon salt, or to taste
- 6 tablespoons olive oil
  Shaved Parmesan cheese to taste
  Black pepper to taste

Cut the oranges crosswise into 8 slices each. Place in a salad bowl. Halve the cored fennel bulbs lengthwise and cut into medium to thin slices. Place on oranges. Drain the olives and add. Toss lightly.

Combine the vinegar, mustard, and salt in a small bowl and whisk together. Gradually whisk in olive oil. Add 3 table-spoons to the salad and toss, using more if necessary.

Arrange on individual plates and top with shaved Parmesan and a good grind of black pepper.

Serves 6

FENNEL, CELERY, AND PARSLEY SALAD WITH SHAVED PARMESAN

This combination, minced and minus the cheese, is a nice little dish to serve with fish. Try it. Guests often don't know what it is. They recognize the tastes, but are puzzled.

- 2¼ cups thinly sliced fennel
- 2¼ cups thinly sliced celery
- 1¼ cups minced fresh parsley
  Shaved Parmesan cheese to taste
  Black pepper to taste

Toss the fennel, celery, and parsley together. Using the same salad dressing as for the Fennel and Orange Salad, add 3 tablespoons and toss. Add more as necessary. Place on individual serving plates and top with shaved Parmesan and a good grind of black pepper.

Serves 6

ABOVE: *Farmhouse entrance.* OPPOSITE TOP: *Fennel and Orange Salad.* OPPOSITE BOTTOM: *Fennel, Celery, and Parsley Salad.*

Two Old-Fashioned Desserts and One Surprise

HAZELNUT SHORTBREAD

I make shortbread of some kind almost everywhere I stay because it keeps so well and is so good with ice cream, tea, and any kind of fruit.

- 1 **cup sugar**
- 1¼ **cups all-purpose flour**
  Pinch of salt
- 1 **cup coarsely chopped, lightly toasted hazelnuts**
- 1 **cup (2 sticks) unsalted butter, softened**
- 1 **teaspoon vanilla extract**

Preheat the oven to 350 degrees. Butter two 8-inch square baking pans.

Combine the sugar, flour, salt, and hazelnuts. Mix with a fork. Add the butter and start to mix with your hands. When combined, sprinkle the vanilla over all and mix thoroughly. Pat into the prepared pans and score the tops to make it easier to cut after baking.

Bake until set and turning slightly golden, about 25 to 30 minutes. Allow to cool for a few minutes before cutting. If shortbread is allowed to cool completely before cutting, you will need to break it apart into serving pieces.
Makes about 18 squares

ABOVE: *Lavender on the hill.* OPPOSITE: *Hazelnut Shortbread.*

POACHED PLUMS AND CHERRIES

This basic poaching liquid may be used to cook any combination of fruit.

- 2 cups cold water
- 2 cups sugar
- 12 peppercorns
- 2 cinnamon sticks (optional)
- 8 whole cloves (optional)
- 2 cups dry white wine
- 12 assorted plums
- 1 cup fresh cherries, with stems if possible

Combine water and sugar in a pot large enough to hold the fruit. Simmer over medium heat until the sugar is dissolved, then add peppercorns, cinnamon sticks, and cloves. Simmer over lowest heat for another 5 minutes. Add wine, increase heat and bring to a light boil. Add fruit, and simmer until it is just tender, about 3 to 5 minutes, depending on the age and kind of fruit. Do not overcook.

Remove fruit to a glass bowl with a slotted spoon. When cool, remove loosened plum skins if desired. Do not try to skin cherries. Meanwhile, reduce the poaching liquid over high heat until thickened slightly, about 15 minutes. Cool and pour over fruit.

Chill and serve with shortbread.
Serves 6 to 8

PEACHES AND FRESH PECORINO WITH HONEY AND BLACK PEPPER

I had something similar to this in a restaurant once. Now I like to serve it after a pasta that has no cheese on it.

You must use only *fresh* pecorino for this, not aged. If fresh is not available, substitute Gruyère.

6 **medium-thick slices fresh pecorino cheese**
3 **medium peaches, skinned, halved, and rubbed with lemon juice**
 Black pepper to taste
 Approximately 4 tablespoons honey

Arrange the slices of cheese on individual plates with a half-peach each. Grind black pepper over all and spoon honey over each.
Serves 6

LEFT: *Poached Plums and Cherries.* ABOVE: *The surprise—Peaches and Fresh Pecorino with Honey and Black Pepper.*

A Crostini Lunch

MY FIRST ENCOUNTER with crostini was on my first visit to Italy in 1955, and it was love at first taste. There are actually several ways of making them. Sometimes the filling is put between two slices of bread and then toasted. This is very good, but I like the simpler method — just spreading the filling on the top of a piece of grilled, toasted, or fried bread. The most classic topping is made with chicken livers, but I suspect almost anything goes. Making crostini is probably a tasty way to clean out the refrigerator.

Whatever, I like to put the toasted bread, sometimes rubbed with garlic and then brushed with olive oil (this depends on my guests' tolerance for garlic), in a basket on the table with all the toppings and let everyone compose whatever they like from it. The Dagwood approach to dining seems right at home here. You can sit for hours — sipping, talking, and nibbling.

Put out a bowl of peaches and pears for dessert, with a few walnuts, or nuts layered with cheese, and you'll be at the table until time for your nap.

CROSTINI WITH ASSORTED TOPPINGS

**PEACHES AND PEARS
WITH SOFT WALNUT GORGONZOLA**

Table set with the fixings for a crostini lunch.

CROSTINI WITH ASSORTED TOPPINGS

Just let your imagination go here and make any sort of topping you like — from tuna mashed with capers and onion to cheese grated into piquant mayonnaise.

Although making bread in Italy is certainly not necessary, I have a wonderful recipe from Texas given to me by Tom Booth, who got it from his father, Brown. It doesn't require real kneading and is great toasted — just what you need here.

BROWN BOOTH'S BREAD

You must make the sourdough mix for this bread at least 24 hours in advance. The only thing hard about this recipe is explaining how to handle the dough, which is very sticky — and that's not even crucial. You might also make this into a round loaf, baking it on an oiled cookie sheet.

- 1 cup warm water, about 105 degrees
- 1 package active dry yeast
- ½ teaspoon sugar
- 3 cups all-purpose flour
- 2 teaspoons salt
- 2 tablespoons vegetable oil
- 1 cup sourdough mix (see *Note*)

Put the water in a small bowl, sprinkle yeast over, and stir in sugar. Allow to stand until foamy, about 5 minutes.

Generously oil two 8½ x 4½-inch loaf pans with olive oil. Set aside.

Pour yeast into a large bowl and mix with all other ingredients. When well combined, spread additional flour on a clean surface and turn the dough out onto it. Sprinkle the flour over the top and work a bit more into the sides. Roll it around to make a long sausage shape approximately the length of the oiled pans. Brush off excess flour, divide dough in half, and place in the 2 pans. The dough is very damp so you aren't really kneading it in the conventional sense, but rather just pressing a bit of flour into it and flopping it around.

Wildflower bouquet.

Allow dough in the pans to rise in a warm, draft-free spot until it comes near the tops of the pans, about 30 minutes or more. If you have an oven kept warm by a pilot light, that is a good place in which to allow the dough to rise.

Preheat the oven to 400 degrees and bake until golden brown on top, about 30 minutes.
Makes 2 loaves

Note: Make sourdough mix by combining equal amounts of flour and water. Allow to stand uncovered at least 24 hours before using. You may keep this mix going by adding more flour and water to the mixture as you use it and stirring occasionally.

TOMATO AND BASIL TOPPING

Some people add a little minced garlic to this, but I like it better without. Suit yourself. If anything, I'd add shallots.

- 4 medium tomatoes, peeled, seeded, and coarsely chopped
- 1 small onion, minced
- 12 large fresh basil leaves, minced
  Salt and black pepper to taste

Toss all ingredients together and let stand at room temperature.

CHICKEN LIVER TOPPING

Many people have a favorite recipe for chicken livers. If you are one of those, use your own. But if you use this one, use *fresh* sage.

- 1 tablespoon olive oil
- 1 tablespoon unsalted butter
- ¾ cup minced onion
- ½ pound chicken livers, chopped
- 1 tablespoon finely chopped fresh sage
- 1 tablespoon minced fresh parsley
- 1 tablespoon Marsala wine
- 1 teaspoon lemon juice
- ½ teaspoon salt
- ¼ teaspoon black pepper

Heat the oil and butter in a skillet over medium-high heat. Sauté the onion for 5 minutes. Add chicken livers and stir. Continue to cook for another 2 minutes, then add sage. Cook 2 minutes and add parsley, Marsala, lemon juice, salt, and pepper. Cook another 3 minutes. All traces of pink should be gone from the chicken livers, but they should still be moist and spreadable. Correct seasoning with additional salt, pepper, or Marsala if necessary.
Makes about 1½ cups

EGGS IN PIQUANT MAYONNAISE

The recipe for this piquant mayonnaise came from Silvestro Baraldo, who is the chef and owner of the popular Bar Centrale on the square in San Casciano dei Bagni.

When I make this, I usually double the piquant mayonnaise recipe to have extra to use on sandwiches.

- ¾ cup Homemade Mayonnaise (page 34)
- 2 tablespoons hot pepper oil (see *Note*)
- ½ teaspoon Worcestershire sauce
- 2 teaspoons lemon juice
- 3 eggs, hard-cooked and chopped fine

Whisk together the mayonnaise, hot pepper oil, Worcestershire sauce, and lemon juice. Fold in eggs.
Makes 1¼ cups

Note: Silvestro makes hot pepper oil by heating the fiery small dried *pepperoncini* (peppers) in olive oil and then allowing them to steep. Chinese hot pepper oil could be substituted here.

SWEET BELL PEPPER AND ONION

I use several colors of peppers for this, but that is mostly because I like the way it looks. Sweet red peppers alone would do fine.

- 2 tablespoons olive oil
- 2 tablespoons unsalted butter
- 1 medium onion, coarsely chopped
- 2 medium garlic cloves, minced
- 1 large yellow bell pepper, seeded and diced
- 1 large red bell pepper, seeded and diced
- ¼ cup water or stock

In a large skillet, heat the oil and butter over medium heat and sauté the onion until slightly wilted, about 5 minutes. Add the garlic and sauté another minute or so. Add peppers and water. Cover and cook over low heat until peppers are soft, about 30 minutes, stirring occasionally.
Makes about 1½ cups

ANCHOVIES, CAPERS, BASIL, AND PINE NUTS

You may also add a few black olives to this if you like.

- 16 flat anchovy filets, drained
  Generous ¼ cup drained capers
  Generous ¼ cup minced fresh basil
  Generous ¼ cup pine nuts
- 2 teaspoons lemon juice
- 2 tablespoons olive oil

Mince the anchovies, capers, basil, and nuts together by hand, then stir in the lemon juice and oil. Or put all the ingredients in a small food processor and chop it together; care should be taken not to overprocess the mixture. The finished paste should be coarse.
Makes about 1 cup

SAUTEED MUSHROOMS

Of course in Italy we use wild mushrooms, which don't require much attention. Milder mushrooms might be more flavorful with a dash of Tabasco and a small quantity of Worcestershire sauce. This also may be cooked with minced parsley.

- 3 tablespoons olive oil
- 1 tablespoon unsalted butter
- 3 cups very coarsely chopped mushrooms, caps and stems
- 1½ teaspoons fresh lemon juice
  Salt and pepper to taste

Heat the oil and butter in a large skillet. Add the mushrooms and sauté over medium heat until they give up most of their liquid and are tender, about 10 to 15 minutes. Add lemon juice and season to taste.
Makes 2 cups plus

CUCUMBER BUTTER

The trick to this very uncomplicated but tasty butter is to get the cucumbers dry enough.

- ½ large cucumber, peeled, seeded, chopped, and lightly salted
- ½ cup (1 stick) unsalted butter, softened
- ¼ teaspoon lemon juice
  Salt (optional)

Let the salted chopped cucumber stand in a colander for about 30 minutes, then squeeze as much liquid from it as possible. One way of doing this is to dump the drained cucumber onto a tea towel, fold the towel over, and twist it as if you were wringing it out.

Whip the cucumber pulp into the butter along with the lemon juice. Add salt if desired.
Makes about ¾ cup

PARSLEY PINE-NUT BUTTER

This tangy butter would be very good on simple broiled fish with just a bit of lemon and black pepper.

- 1½ cups loosely packed parsley leaves
  Generous ¼ cup pine nuts
- 1 large garlic clove, cut into several pieces
- ¼ teaspoon salt
- 3 tablespoons olive oil
- ½ cup (1 stick) unsalted butter, softened

Place the parsley, pine nuts, garlic, and salt in a small food processor. Pulse until mixture is coarsely chopped, then continue to process, adding olive oil, until smooth. Beat into softened butter.
Makes about ¾ cup

Dinner on the "Afternoon" Terrace

Every once in a while we decide to cook a more substantial meal at the house and sit down like "grown-ups" to something similar to what we are accustomed to having back home. This menu, though certainly showing its Italian bent, is one of those.

The main dish utilizes a mushroom broth which is a very handy thing to know how to make since it can be used anywhere as the basis for anything from soups to sauces.

**PASTA SHELLS AND JULIENNE PORK IN
MUSHROOM BROTH**

GARDEN SALAD WITH FONTINA CHEESE

ALMOND AND RICOTTA TART WITH PEARS

ABOVE: *Flowers gathered by the roadside.* RIGHT: *Table set for dinner.*

PASTA SHELLS AND JULIENNE PORK IN MUSHROOM BROTH

This dish may be made with beef or veal, too. In fact, we had hoped to get wild boar, which is often available in Tuscany. But no luck.

4	cups thinly sliced white mushrooms, including stems
1½	cups thinly sliced shallots
3	cups thinly sliced onions
3	large garlic cloves, thinly sliced
4	cups water
	Salt and black pepper to taste
1¼	to 1½ pounds boneless pork loin, trimmed of all fat and cut into ¼-inch-thick slices
3	tablespoons flour
4	tablespoons olive oil
4	cups chicken stock
1	tablespoon lemon juice
½	pound small pasta shells

Place the mushrooms, shallots, onions, and garlic in a large, heavy skillet, preferably nonstick without any oil, and cook over medium-high heat, stirring, for about 5 minutes, until mushrooms begin to give up liquid. Continue to cook over medium heat, stirring, for another 15 minutes to reduce. Do not allow to burn. Add water and reduce over medium heat for another 30 minutes. Strain out solids, reserving ½ cup and discarding the rest. You should have about 1¼ to 1⅓ cups of liquid. Refrigerate mushroom liquid and reserved solids separately until ready to use. This may be done several days in advance.

Place the reserved mushroom solids and liquid in a food processor and puree mixture. Pour into a nonreactive pot and set aside.

Salt and generously pepper the pork slices and then dredge them in flour, shaking off excess. Heat olive oil in a large skillet and fry pork slices about 3 minutes per side, until turning golden (add another tablespoon of olive oil if necessary). Cut pork into ¼-inch julienne strips and set aside.

Pour out any oil remaining in the skillet and deglaze with the chicken stock, scraping and dissolving pan solids. Stir in mushroom mixture and heat. Correct seasoning with additional salt and pepper, and lemon juice. Add pork julienne and set aside off heat.

Cook the pasta shells according to package directions and drain. Divide among 6 warm soup bowls. Reheat the pork and liquid quickly and ladle over the pasta shells.

Serves 6

GARDEN SALAD WITH FONTINA CHEESE

Any combination of garden greens is fine here.

8	cups loosely packed mixed garden greens, well washed, dried, and torn into bite-size bits
¾	teaspoon salt
	Black pepper to taste
1	heaping teaspoon Dijon-style mustard
3	tablespoons red wine or balsamic vinegar
6	tablespoons olive oil
6	small wedges fontina cheese

Place greens in a bowl, cover with a tea towel, and refrigerate.

Combine salt, pepper, mustard, and vinegar. Whisk. Add oil, continuing to whisk until well combined.

Add 2 tablespoons of the vinaigrette to the greens and toss to coat leaves. Add more vinaigrette as desired.

Serve with a wedge of cheese.

Serves 6

OPPOSITE: *Pasta Shells and Julienne Pork in Mushroom Broth.* BELOW: *Garden Salad with Fontina Cheese.*

ALMOND AND RICOTTA TART WITH PEARS

This is an adaptation of a classic Italian tart, not too sweet and rather thin. It's ideal with soft ice cream, flavored whipped cream, or fruit.

- ¼ cup fine bread crumbs, toasted
- 2 large eggs
- ½ cup sugar
- 1 cup ricotta cheese
- ½ cup coarsely chopped toasted almonds
  Pinch of salt
- ¼ teaspoon almond extract
- 1 teaspoon vanilla extract

Generously butter a 10- to 11-inch tart pan then coat it with the toasted bread crumbs. Set aside and preheat the oven to 350 degrees.

Beat the eggs and sugar together until well blended, then beat in ricotta. Fold in almonds. Add salt and extracts. Mix well and pour into prepared pan.

Bake until golden and puffy, about 30 to 35 minutes. Allow to cool. Serve at room temperature with poached pears (recipe follows).
Serves 6 to 8

POACHED PEARS

- 2 cups sugar
- 2 cups cold water
- 4 firm pears, peeled, cored, and cut into medium chunks
- 1 large lemon, juiced

Combine sugar and water in a small, deep pot. Bring quickly to a boil. Add pears and bring quickly back to a boil. When boiling add lemon juice and cook pears until just tender, about 7 minutes, depending on the age and ripeness of the pears. Skim as necessary.

Remove pears to a bowl and reduce the syrup over high heat until thick, about 15 minutes. Pour over pears and allow to cool. Refrigerate covered.
Serves 6

ABOVE: *Almond and Ricotta Tart with Pears.* RIGHT: *Tuscan countryside.*

Bonus Recipes

Here are some dishes that don't fit into any particular menu but that are simply too good to pass up. You can mix them with your regular menus or you can build a meal around them. Anything goes!

THE TUSCAN SANDWICH

Actually this is no more a Tuscan sandwich than I am, but I call it that because here is where I make it, and because grilling was a way of cooking in Tuscany long before — by at least a thousand years — it was made so *wildly* chic in California.

You are likely to find grilling facilities in most country houses here — new and old, inside and outside. For instance, the fireplace in the dining room is often raised for this purpose. It is built that way in the house where we stay.

You can put any number of grilled elements in my Tuscan sandwich — mushrooms, onions, and seeded tomato slices. Make it with or without cheese. However, after experimenting with others, I've decided I like the version here the best.

8 thick lengthwise slices from several large zucchini
8 thick lengthwise slices from 2 medium eggplants
   Olive oil
   Balsamic vinegar
2 large red bell peppers, roasted, peeled, and seeded
4 slices Italian bread, about ¼ inch thick, generously rubbed on one side with garlic and brushed well with olive oil
8 medium slices mozzarella cheese
   Salt and pepper to taste
   Thin Fried Onions (page 27)

Rub zucchini and eggplant slices with olive oil and then sprinkle with vinegar. Set aside. Cut peppers into wide strips and set aside. Grill the zucchini and eggplant about 6 inches from the coals until tender and turning golden, about 4 or more minutes on each side. (This timing is only approximate, since it will ultimately depend on how close the vegetables are to the heat and how hot the coals are.) Set aside. Grill the bread, bare side down first, until lightly toasted. Turn and grill the oiled side.

Assemble the sandwiches by layering the eggplant, pepper, and zucchini on each slice of the grilled bread, oiled side up. Salt and pepper the layers to taste. Top with mozzarella and run the sandwiches under the broiler just long enough to melt the cheese slightly. Place on individual plates and sprinkle with the fried onions and serve immediately.
Serves 4

LEFT: *Tuscan Sandwich.* OPPO-
SITE: *Lavender.* BELOW: *On the
crest of a Tuscan hill.*

91

ADRIANA'S GNOCCHI

Adriana is the maid in the house we visit in Tuscany, and she often makes this dish for us for supper. I'd never made gnocchi in my life, but I liked hers so much I got her to teach me. Serve this with a glass of wine and any salad. It makes a perfect light meal.

Once you find how easy it is to make gnocchi, maybe you will go on to experiment with other sauces instead of having it with the cheese only. Gnocchi is, of course, sublime with porcini sauce.

> 2   cups milk
> 2   cups water
> ½   teaspoon salt
> 6   tablespoons unsalted butter
> 1   cup semolina
> ½   cup grated Parmesan cheese

Tear off a sheet of foil about 2 feet long, lay it on the counter, and butter it well. Butter a 9x12-inch baking dish and set it aside.

Combine the milk, water, salt, and 4 tablespoons butter in a saucepan and heat, without boiling. When butter is melted, start stirring in the semolina. When all the semolina is in the pot, turn up the heat and bring to a slow boil, stirring. Cook, stirring, until smooth and thick, about 30 minutes. Pour out onto buttered foil and smooth to a thickness of slightly less than ½ inch. Allow to cool and set, about 1 hour.

Cut semolina into 2-inch squares and place in buttered dish, touching.

Dot with the remaining 2 tablespoons of butter and sprinkle with the Parmesan. This may be put aside for a few hours at this point, covered with a tea towel but not refrigerated.

Preheat the oven to 350 degrees and bake the gnocchi until golden and bubbly, about 50 to 60 minutes.
Serves 6

—

STUFFED CREPES WITH RED BELL PEPPER SAUCE

I always thought it was too much trouble to make crepes until a friend, who is a professional, showed me how simple they are to prepare. They may be made in advance and stowed in the refrigerator all day, or if you really get a head of steam up, you can make a big batch and freeze them separated by waxed paper.

Any other strong-flavored green, such as broccoli rabe, spinach, chickory, or Swiss chard, could be substituted for the escarole.

CREPES

- 2 large eggs
- 1 cup milk
- ½ cup water
- 2 teaspoons unsalted butter, melted
- 1 teaspoon salt
- ⅔ cup all-purpose flour

FILLING

- 6 tablespoons unsalted butter
- 1 cup finely chopped onion
- 4 cups lightly packed stemmed escarole
- ½ cup chicken stock
- 1 teaspoon salt
- ¼ teaspoon pepper
- ¼ teaspoon grated nutmeg
- 1 cup ricotta cheese
- 1¼ cups grated Parmesan cheese
- 1 large egg
  Red Bell Pepper Sauce (page 72)

Make the crepes: Place egg, milk, water, butter, and salt in a bowl and whip it with a fork until smooth. Sprinkle flour over all while continuing to beat with a fork; when smooth set aside.

Using additional butter lightly rub the inside of a 7-inch crêpe or omelet pan. Heat over high heat. Pour ¼ cup of the batter into the pan and cook until top is no longer shiny, loosening it around the edges with your spatula as it cooks, about 1½ minutes. Turn and lightly brown other side, another 1½ minutes. Set crepe aside. Repeat until all batter is used, wiping out the pan with a paper towel and rebuttering it after each crepe. Place a paper towel between finished crepes. If you are not using these right away, separate crepes with waxed paper.

Make the filling: Melt 2 tablespoons butter over medium-high heat and sauté onion and escarole until wilted, about 5 minutes. Add stock and cook until it is almost entirely evaporated, about 6 to 8 minutes. Place in a strainer and gently press out any remaining liquid. Chop coarsely and set aside. Combine salt, pepper, and nutmeg with the ricotta, ½ cup Parmesan, and egg. Mix well and fold in the chopped escarole.

OPPOSITE TOP: *Adriana.* OPPOSITE BOTTOM: *Adriana's Gnocchi.* ABOVE: *Stuffed Crepes with Red Bell Pepper Sauce.*

Preheat the oven to 350 degrees.

Spread 1 generous tablespoon of the filling over the bottom half of a crepe, leaving a ¼-inch border around the lower edge. Fold top half over filling and press down lightly. Fold over one more time, making a triangle with a rounded side. Repeat.

Place crepes in 1 or 2 buttered baking dishes and sprinkle each crepe with 1 tablespoon of remaining Parmesan and dot it with ½ teaspoon of remaining butter. Cover tightly with foil and bake for 30 minutes. Uncover and bake until just beginning to turn golden, about 10 more minutes.

Allow 2 crepes per serving, placing them on heated plates with some Red Bell Pepper Sauce.

Serves 6

In Gascony

S EVERAL YEARS AGO I spent a greater part of spring and summer tooling around California's Napa and Sonoma counties. Since this is where all that extraordinary wine — and food — comes from, I had a pretty good time for myself and along the way got to know lots of people in the wine business. Among them was a marvelous lady who had inherited her family's chateau near L'Isle Jourdain, in Gascony — about a thirty-minute drive from Toulouse. She was interested in food, so naturally we got along swimmingly. At some point I mentioned I'd probably be in Italy with a group of friends the following year, so she suggested that we might like to hop over to France for a weekend while we were there.

How could I pass up the opportunity not only to visit the house but to see, however briefly, a part of France I'd never been to before? I didn't resist.

Frankly, all I knew about the region was that it is the source of cassoulet and foie gras — rich stuff I grant you, but I figured I could force myself to at least taste it. Especially with armagnac, Gascony's other great indigenous inspiration, to look forward to after dinner.

You can see how the weekend was shaping up in my mind.

Anyway, within easy driving distance from the chateau were *two* two-star restaurants, Hôtel de France and L'Aubergade. Since this gastronomic lagniappe meant we'd be dining out at least two evenings, and since we food nuts were bound to cook at least one

meal together during our stay, we finally settled on doing a sumptuous picnic on our last day.

Now about the two restaurants. When you come to Gascony you absolutely must get to the Hôtel de France. You have never had foie gras until you have tried one of chef-owner André Daguin's dozen or so variations.

OPPOSITE: *A picnic under the trees.*
ABOVE: *Chateau roses.*

These change regularly, but I'm told they're consistently sublime. The ones we had certainly were. Dining at the Hôtel de France was exactly what eating in such an establishment is supposed to be. Obviously it was about superb food, but it was also about epicurean style, welcoming ease, flawless service, and comfort. These qualities are frequently woefully lacking in their highly touted American *faux* equivalents, where the whole experience is too often charged with arrogance.

Finally, about L'Aubergade. Alas, it was a big disappointment.

A Sumptuous
Picnic

W<small>E WANTED</small> to try a few of the "house recipes" —
two of which were gratins — for our picnic, which
we planned to set out under an ancient tree on the
property. The gratins weren't strictly picnic fare (or
so it seemed), but I loved the sound of them and was anxious to
taste them. It turns out they were terrific for our picnic. I'm very
partial to food that can be served just warm, and these were delicious this way.

GARLIC-ROASTED CHICKEN

HAM "CAKE"

SLOW-BAKED TOMATOES

STUFFED ARTICHOKE BOTTOMS

EGGPLANT AND TUNA GRATIN

POTATO AND CABBAGE GRATIN

ARMAGNAC AND PRUNE ICE CREAM

ABOVE: *Garlic-Roasted Chicken, Ham "Cake," and Stuffed Artichoke Bottoms.* TOP RIGHT: *Garden urn.* RIGHT: *View of the chateau tower.*

GARLIC-ROASTED CHICKEN

We used two small chickens, but one large one would do.

> 2 medium to small chickens, about 6 pounds total
> Olive oil
> Salt and pepper to taste
> 3 large garlic heads

Preheat the oven to 450 degrees.

Rub the chicken well with olive oil. Sprinkle inside and out with salt and pepper. Peel 2 whole heads of garlic and put an equal number of peeled cloves in each chicken.

Place on a rack and separate the cloves of the third head of garlic. Sprinkle them, unpeeled, around in the bottom of the roasting pan. Roast for 15 minutes before turning oven back to 350 degrees. Continue roasting, basting several times, until golden and juices run clear, about 45 to 50 minutes total roasting time.

Serve warm or at room temperature. The garlic roasted in the pan may be squeezed out and spread on bread to eat with the chicken if you like.
Serves 6 to 8

HAM "CAKE"

This may also be made using Emmental cheese.

> 1 cup all-purpose flour
> 3 large eggs, lightly beaten
> ½ cup milk
> ½ cup peanut oil
> Pinch of salt and pepper
> 2 cups pea-size cubes cooked ham
> 2 cups grated Gruyère cheese
> 1 package active dry yeast

Preheat the oven to 350 degrees. Butter a 4x10-inch loaf pan.

Mix thoroughly the flour, eggs, milk, oil, salt, and pepper. Fold in the ham and cheese. Sprinkle yeast over the top and mix well. Pour into prepared pan. Bake until golden, about 1 hour. If any oil oozes out, pour it off. Serve lukewarm or toasted.
Makes 1 loaf

SLOW-BAKED TOMATOES

These may also be chopped coarsely with fresh basil or tarragon and tossed with pasta.

> 5 tablespoons peanut oil
> 8 medium tomatoes
> 2 teaspoons sugar
> ½ teaspoon salt
> ¼ teaspoon pepper
> 3 medium garlic cloves, minced
> 1 tablespoon olive oil
> ½ cup minced fresh parsley

Preheat the oven to 300 degrees.

Spread oil in a jelly roll pan. Cut off one-third of the stem end of the tomatoes. Discard the cut-off ends. Place tomatoes in the pan, cut side down, and bake for 30 minutes. Turn and bake for another 30 minutes, basting with the pan juices occasionally. Sprinkle with the sugar, salt, and pepper. Cook for another 1½ hours until tomatoes are flattened.

Sauté garlic in the olive oil over medium heat until soft, about 4 minutes. Do not brown. Stir in parsley and sprinkle over cooked tomatoes.
Serves 8

STUFFED ARTICHOKE BOTTOMS

It's important to rub the artichokes with lemon juice as you trim them so they won't turn dark.

> 2 medium lemons
> 8 medium artichokes, leaves snapped off and edges trimmed, chokes removed
> 3 cups pitted and chopped oil-cured black olives
> 12 anchovy filets, drained and coarsely chopped
> ¾ cup capers
> ¾ cup coarsely chopped fresh parsley
> 3 medium garlic cloves
> 3 hard-cooked eggs, finely chopped
> ¼ cup olive oil
> Black pepper to taste

Use one of the lemons to rub artichokes as you trim them, dropping each artichoke into a saucepan of water into which you have squeezed the other lemon. When all artichokes are trimmed, bring the water to a boil and cook over medium heat until artichoke bottoms are tender, about 50 minutes. Remove with a slotted spoon and allow to cool.

Meanwhile combine all the other ingredients except the eggs, olive oil, and pepper. Chop and toss lightly to combine the flavors. Do not chop too fine. Mix with the egg and oil, adding pepper and more oil if desired. Top artichoke bottoms with equal amounts of the mixture, using it all.
Serves 8

RIGHT: *Slow-Baked Tomatoes.* OPPO-SITE: *Potato Cabbage Gratin and Eggplant and Tuna Gratin.* OVERLEAF: *Hollyhocks.*

EGGPLANT AND TUNA GRATIN

This could be served as a supper dish followed by a green salad and fruit.

- 3 medium eggplants
  Salt
- 6 tablespoons olive oil
- 1½ cups coarsely chopped onions
- 2 cups coarsely chopped, peeled, and seeded tomatoes
- 2 tablespoons minced garlic
- ⅓ cup minced fresh parsley
- 2 6½-ounce cans tuna in oil, drained and crumbled
- ½ teaspoon salt, or to taste
  Pinch of black pepper
- 2 teaspoons paprika
- 2 large eggs, lightly beaten
- ¾ cup grated Emmental cheese

Preheat the oven to 350 degrees.

Cut off and discard the stem and blossom ends of the eggplants. Cut into thick slices lengthwise, sprinkle with salt, and set out the slices on paper towels to drain.

Heat 2 tablespoons of the olive oil in a large skillet over medium heat. Add the onions and tomatoes. Sauté until soft, about 5 minutes. Add the garlic and parsley. Mix thoroughly and transfer to a bowl. Add the tuna to the onion-tomato mixture along with the salt, pepper, paprika, and eggs. Set aside.

Wipe out skillet and put in the balance of the oil. Wipe off eggplant and fry over very high heat until tender and slightly golden, about 3 minutes per side. Add more oil if necessary.

Lightly oil an 8x10-inch gratin dish and arrange a layer of eggplant on the bottom. Top this with a layer of the tuna mixture. Continue making layers until all is used, ending with eggplant. Sprinkle with the cheese and bake until the cheese is melted and turning golden, about 30 to 35 minutes.
Serves 8

POTATO AND CABBAGE GRATIN

This may also be topped with parboiled cubes of bacon before it is baked.

- 6 cups finely shredded green cabbage
- 2 cups Light Béchamel Sauce (recipe follows)
- 3 cups cooked, peeled, and sliced red potatoes
- 1 cup shredded Gruyère cheese
  Salt and pepper to taste
- 2 tablespoons unsalted butter

Place cabbage in a large saucepan of salted water and boil over medium heat for 2 minutes. Drain and cover with cold water, bring back to a simmer (this takes about 20 minutes), and cook for 30 minutes over medium heat.

Meanwhile, preheat the oven to 350 degrees and lightly grease an 8-inch round gratin dish.

Spread ⅔ cup of the Béchamel in the bottom of the dish. Layer half of the cooked cabbage, top with half the potato slices and half of the Gruyère, sprinkling each layer with salt and pepper as you go. Pour over another ⅔ cup of the Béchamel. Make a final layer using balance of the ingredients and ending with Béchamel. Dot with butter, cover with foil, and bake for 15 minutes. Remove foil and bake until light golden and bubbly, 30 to 40 minutes more.
Serves 8

LIGHT BECHAMEL SAUCE

You may use your own Béchamel sauce recipe or the one below, which calls for less milk and butter.

- 2 tablespoons unsalted butter
- 2 tablespoons minced shallots
- 1½ to 2 tablespoons flour
- 2 cups low-fat milk, or half milk and half chicken stock
- ½ teaspoon salt or to taste
- ¼ teaspoon pepper or to taste

Melt butter over medium-high heat and sauté shallots, stirring, until they begin to brown, 2 to 3 minutes. Stir in flour and cook, stirring constantly, for about 1 minute. Meanwhile, heat the 2 cups of liquid. Whisk into the butter-flour roux, and add the salt and pepper. Bring to a boil, then turn heat back to medium and continue cooking, whisking, until it begins to thicken, about 5 minutes. You want a pourable sauce about the consistency of heavy cream; add more liquid if it is too thick.
Makes 2 cups

ARMAGNAC AND PRUNE ICE CREAM

In some versions of this local favorite the prunes are pureed before adding. I prefer the prunes to be a little coarser than the usual puree. Either way, it is delicious.

It is best to prepare the prunes in advance, since they must macerate in tea, be drained, and then macerate in armagnac. If you have time, macerate the prunes in the liquor overnight.

    1   cup minced pitted prunes
    1   cup strong hot tea
    ⅓   cup armagnac
    1   cup milk
    ⅔   cup sugar
    2   vanilla beans, cut in half
        lengthwise
    9   large egg yolks, at room
        temperature
    2   cups heavy cream

Cover the prunes with the tea and set aside for at least 6 hours. Drain the prunes and cover with the armagnac. Allow to macerate overnight if you can,
but for at least three hours.

Combine the milk, sugar, and vanilla beans in the top of a double boiler and heat over barely simmering water. Lightly beat the yolks. When the milk mixture is almost to the point of boiling, pour a little into the yolks to warm them. Stir and add a bit more milk. Pour warmed yolks into the milk in a slow, steady stream, stirring all the while. Continue to cook, stirring constantly over hot, not boiling, water until mixture coats the spoon.

Press a sheet of waxed paper or plastic wrap directly onto the surface of the custard and allow it to cool to room temperature.

Add the cream to the custard and refrigerate for several hours. Just before freezing, remove the vanilla beans and scrape their seeds into the mixture. Stir the prunes into the mixture along with the armagnac. These may also be pureed before adding to the cream. Pour into an ice-cream maker and freeze according to the manufacturer's directions.
Makes 1 generous quart

ABOVE: *Armagnac and Prune Ice Cream.* RIGHT: *An ancient topiary overlooks the field.*

ABOVE: *Gâteau Norman.*
OPPOSITE: *Me and morning coffee.*

Breakfast in a Chateau

I'VE LOVED *café au lait* ever since I was a child, when it was more coffee-flavored milk than the real thing. But this child's version set my taste for it early. On this visit to France, maybe being able to gaze out the window of a real chateau while drinking my *café au lait* is what made this old favorite so special. Whatever, along with the usual croissants, rolls, jams, and butter, breakfast coffee was served with a tempting sort of apple tart called Gâteau Norman. It turns out to be extremely uncomplicated to make. So here it is.

GATEAU NORMAN

This may also be made with pears.

- 3 tart apples, peeled, cored, and quartered
- 2 tablespoons lemon juice
- 1 tablespoon grated lemon rind
- ¾ cup all-purpose flour
- ⅔ cup sugar
- ½ cup milk
- 2 tablespoons vegetable oil
- ½ package active dry yeast
- 6 tablespoons unsalted butter, melted
- 1 large egg, lightly beaten

Preheat the oven to 350 degrees. Butter a 10-inch tart pan and set aside.

Place quartered apples in a small bowl. Toss apples with 1 tablespoon of the lemon juice and set aside. Combine the tablespoon of grated rind with another tablespoon of the juice and mix.

Mix flour and ⅓ cup of sugar. Stir in the milk, vegetable oil, and reserved lemon juice and rind. Sprinkle the yeast over all and mix. Spoon into the prepared pan. Arrange apples, rounded side up, on the mixture.

Combine remaining sugar, melted butter, and egg. Spoon this over the apples. Bake until apples are tender and cake is puffy, about 25 to 30 minutes.

This may be served as a dessert by topping with flavored whipped cream or ice cream.

Serves 6

In the
Hamptons

THINKING IT OVER, I suppose I could say that my cooking "career" began in earnest in the Hamptons. My childhood and the time I lived in New Orleans helped define my taste in food, but it was in my Bridgehampton kitchen that I really got going. Although I did start cooking seriously in New Orleans, these attempts were what I now think of as my pretentious period — "high" French recipes, wildly complicated and way beyond my untutored capabilities (and my untutored palate). You see, I had to grow up a bit before I could really appreciate my roots.

By the late 50s I had returned to New York City and with a group of friends had rented my first beach house in Quogue. Out there we all got into cooking and for large groups. There wasn't much time for food phoniness, or even subtlety, thank heaven.

Then when I finally was able to build my own house, the pace quickened. During those years in the new digs a close friend spent

ABOVE: *Day lilies.* RIGHT: *Fall produce.*

her summers with me, and she was always taking pictures with her newfangled Polaroid camera. Like all people with a new house at the beach, we thought we weren't really having fun unless all the beds were filled and the place was overflowing at mealtimes. Recently, though, we were looking over these snapshots and the remark second only to how obscenely young we all looked was, "Who is *that?*"

Well, things quieted down over the years.

When I moved into the house, my taste in food was pretty much what it should have been all along, although I suppose you have to have *some* understanding of classic cuisine to value the cooking of your past. So those New Orleans years weren't exactly wasted.

Along with my renewed appreciation of familiar food, I had also begun to define what I did and didn't like about cooking and entertaining in general, because actually all the cooking I ever did was to "entertain." I never had to cook three squares for a family so I didn't know what that must be like, but I do know it's probably not the same (except in spirit) as the food I prepare most of the time — except for those meals I cook for myself when I'm at home alone.

So little by little I started to learn about simplicity. And since that's what I had always so firmly believed in in design (and most other things), I imagine this was a natural evolvement.

Here we are years later, still cooking, still entertaining, and still enjoying it — just like my father did before me.

Four Chicken Dinners

I'VE ALWAYS loved chicken. And it's the one thing that seems to please almost everyone. Looking back, I realize I haven't given the old bird its due in my other books. Sure, I know there are chicken recipes sprinkled throughout, but now it's time for me to do a little recipe ode to chicken.

CHICKEN SAUCE PIQUANT

ALMOND PARSLEY RICE

ASPARAGUS VINAIGRETTE

BLACKBERRY JAM TART

CHICKEN SAUCE PIQUANT

If you like your chicken with a very flavorful sauce, this is for you. I love it.

- 1 cup safflower oil
- 2 large chicken breasts, split, with each half cut in half
- 12 chicken thighs
- 1½ cups coarsely chopped onions
- 2 cups coarsely chopped celery
- 1 very large green bell pepper, coarsely chopped
- ¾ cup all-purpose flour
- 4 cups crushed canned tomatoes with juice
- 4 tablespoons tomato paste
- 1 teaspoon Tabasco, or to taste
- 4 cups chicken stock
- 1 tablespoon lemon juice
- 2 large bay leaves
- 2 large garlic cloves, minced
- 1 teaspoon salt
- ½ teaspoon black pepper
- 2 tablespoons chopped green onion tops
- 2 tablespoons finely chopped fresh parsley
- 12 stuffed olives, sliced (optional)

Place the oil in a deep skillet or Dutch oven and brown chicken on all sides, in several batches if necessary. Set aside as browned. Add onion, celery, and green pepper to oil and cook until vegetables are wilted but not browned, about 5 minutes. Remove them with a slotted spoon, draining carefully as you do. Set aside.

Add the flour to the oil and stir over medium heat using a pancake turner, scraping flour from the bottom of the pan as it browns (you are making a roux — see *Note*). When dark brown, stir in tomatoes, tomato paste, Tabasco, chicken stock, lemon juice, bay leaves, garlic, salt, pepper, and reserved vegetables. Bring to a simmer and add the chicken. Simmer, uncovered, for about 1 hour or until chicken is tender and sauce is reduced and thick. When the oil begins to rise and collect on top of the sauce, skim it off and discard.

Mix in green onion tops, parsley, and olives a few minutes before serving. ***Serves 6 to 8, generously***

Note: You should have the tomatoes with their juice and the other liquid ingredients measured and ready to add here. When a roux begins to brown, it burns very quickly; and it will continue to cook — even off the heat — if liquid is not added right away.

———

ALMOND PARSLEY RICE

Chopped toasted pecans are also good in this rice.

- 1 cup long-grain rice, washed
- 3 cups chicken stock
- ½ cup slivered almonds, toasted
- 2 tablespoons unsalted butter
  Salt to taste

Combine the rice and stock in a saucepan and bring to a rolling boil. Turn heat back to medium and boil for 10 minutes. Test for doneness. If not tender, boil for another minute or so. Drain, wash with hot water, and combine with all other ingredients. *Serves 6*

OPPOSITE: ***Chicken Sauce Piquant, Almond Parsley Rice, and Asparagus Vinaigrette.*** BELOW: ***Zinnias and a field of corn.***

ABOVE: *Fall sky.* OPPOSITE:
Blackberry Jam Tart.

ASPARAGUS VINAIGRETTE

When the first very thin (about the size of a pencil), tender asparagus appear in the spring, I cut them into 1-inch pieces and toss them, uncooked, into my green salads.

2 pounds medium asparagus, stems peeled
1 teaspoon salt, or to taste
1 generous teaspoon Dijon-style mustard
  Scant ½ teaspoon black pepper
2 tablespoons balsamic vinegar
3 tablespoons vegetable oil
2 tablespoons olive oil

Bring a large pan of well-salted water to the boil. Put asparagus in and bring back to a boil. Cook until just tender, about 5 minutes. Drain and refresh under cold water.

Arrange the cooled asparagus on a platter or individual plates. Whisk together the remaining ingredients, and spoon vinaigrette over all. Top with an additional grind of pepper.
Serves 6

BLACKBERRY JAM TART

Obviously, you could use any jam you like — blackberry just happens to be a particular favorite of mine.

PASTRY

 1 cup all-purpose flour
 ¼ cup sugar
 ½ teaspoon baking powder
 Salt

 4 tablespoons (½ stick) unsalted butter, chilled
 1 large egg, lightly beaten

FILLING

 6 generous tablespoons blackberry jam
 3 large eggs, separated
 5 tablespoons sugar
 6 tablespoons unsalted butter, melted
 6 tablespoons soft white bread crumbs
 6 tablespoons ground walnuts

Make the pastry: Place flour, sugar, baking powder, and a pinch of salt in a bowl and mix. Cut in the chilled butter with a pastry blender or 2 knives. Stir in egg with a fork to moisten evenly, then gather the pastry together and knead it for a minute or so on a floured surface. Form into a flattened circle and refrigerate, tightly wrapped, for at least 1 hour.

Finish the tart: Preheat the oven to 375 degrees. Roll out the pastry and line bottom and about halfway up the sides of a loose-bottom 9-inch cake pan. Mend any areas that might have broken loose in the process. Spread jam evenly over bottom and set aside.

Beat together the egg yolks, sugar, a pinch of salt, and the melted butter. When thoroughly mixed, stir in the bread crumbs and walnuts. Whip the egg whites until they form stiff peaks and fold into the egg-nut mixture. Spread this evenly over the jam and bake for 30 to 35 minutes or until it has risen and turned slightly golden. Loosen edges and when cooled, slide off onto serving plate.

Serve this plain or with a little thickened cream.
Serves 6 to 8

**CHICKEN PANCAKES WITH
PEACH SALSA**

**CREAMED CORN AND
SWEET PEAS**

**MIXED GREEN SALAD WITH
RASPBERRIES AND RASPBERRY
VINAIGRETTE**

BITTER LEMON TART

CHICKEN PANCAKES
WITH PEACH SALSA

These are also good served with the more traditional sour cream, or crème fraîche.

        Salt and pepper
    6   medium chicken thighs
 1½   cups shredded potato,
        squeezed dry (see *Note*)
    1   small onion, grated
    2   tablespoons flour
   ¾   teaspoon salt
   ¼   teaspoon pepper
        Tabasco to taste

        Vegetable oil and butter for
        frying
    3   medium eggs, lightly beaten

Preheat the oven to 375 degrees.

Generously salt and pepper the chicken thighs and place them skin side up, in a pan into which they fit snugly. Make sure the skin is stretched over all. Bake without opening the door for 30 minutes and then turn off the oven. Leave to be baked by the retained heat for another 45 minutes or so without opening the door. This may be done in advance.

When ready to assemble pancakes, remove skin and bones from the chicken and discard. Chop the meat coarsely. Set aside.

Mix the potato with the onion, flour, salt, pepper, and a drop or two of Tabasco, combining thoroughly.

Place a combination of oil and butter in a large skillet. While this is heating over medium-high heat, combine chicken with potato mixture and then add the eggs. Mix quickly.

When oil is hot, drop rounded table-spoonfuls of the batter into the skillet. Allow to cook until golden, about a minute or so, before turning. Flatten slightly and cook until golden. Keep finished pancakes warm until all the batter is used.
Makes 18 to 24 medium pancakes

Note: To squeeze dry the potato, wrap it in a tea towel and twist out as much liquid as possible.

PEACH SALSA

You may certainly add more green onion and jalapeño pepper to this.

    2   large ripe peaches, about 1
        pound, peeled and pitted
    1   tablespoon fresh lemon or
        lime juice
    2   medium tomatoes, peeled and
        seeded
    6   large green onions, chopped
    1   tablespoon chopped bottled
        jalapeño pepper
    1   tablespoon minced cilantro
        (optional)

12 ears fresh white corn, kernels
cut from cob and scraped
Salt to taste
1 to 2 tablespoons unsalted butter
½ to ¾ cup half-and-half
1 teaspoon sugar
1 cup or more frozen tiny green
peas

Place the kernels in a skillet. Add salt, butter, and enough half-and-half to moisten well. Bring just to a simmer and add sugar. Cook over very low heat until corn is just tender, 5 to 10 minutes. Add more liquid if necessary. (This will depend on how fresh the corn is.)

Meanwhile, place the peas in a strainer. Run hot tap water over them to thaw; do not cook. When the corn is done, stir in the peas and allow to rest a minute until they heat through.
Serves 6

12 tablespoons good olive oil
4 tablespoons sherry vinegar
2 teaspoons honey

Cut the peaches into medium dice and toss with lemon juice. Cut the tomatoes into medium julienne strips.

Combine peaches and tomatoes. Add green onions, jalapeño pepper, and cilantro. Mix. Whisk together oil, vinegar, and honey and pour over the other ingredients.

You may leave this unrefrigerated if you are using it within several hours; otherwise cover it and refrigerate.

Serve with a slotted spoon, allowing most of the juice to drain off.
Makes approximately 3 cups

———

CREAMED CORN
AND SWEET PEAS

I love this little hybrid. Since fresh corn and peas are not in season at the same time in the East, I use small frozen peas. If you live in California you can make the dish with fresh peas.

OPPOSITE: *At the farmstand.*
ABOVE: *Hydrangeas.* BELOW:
Chicken Pancakes with Peach Salsa and Creamed Corn and Sweet Peas.

MIXED GREEN SALAD WITH RASPBERRIES AND RASPBERRY VINAIGRETTE

Use any combination of bitter and mild salad greens you like.

- 6 loosely packed cups mixed salad greens, washed and dried
- ¾ teaspoon salt, or to taste
- 1 scant teaspoon Dijon-style mustard
- 2 tablespoons raspberry vinegar
- 3 tablespoons vegetable oil
- 2 tablespoons olive oil
- ¼ cup fresh raspberries, plus extra for garnish

Place the greens in a salad bowl and set in the refrigerator. Whisk together the salt, mustard, vinegar, and oils. Mash raspberries and stir in. Toss with the greens and arrange on individual salad plates. Garnish with a few whole raspberries.
Serves 6

OPPOSITE: *Mixed Green Salad with Raspberries.* BELOW: *Bitter Lemon Tart.* OVERLEAF: *Pumpkins on parade.*

BITTER LEMON TART

This is one of the desserts my pal Lee Klein passed on to me.

- 2 large lemons
- ½ cup plus 2 tablespoons sugar
- 2 large eggs
  Grated rind of ½ lemon
- 1 partly baked 8-inch pie crust (recipe follows)

The night before, drop the 2 lemons in boiling water, turn off heat, and let stand 5 minutes. Drain and carefully peel, scraping away all the white pith.

Using a very sharp knife, slice the lemons as thin as you can, discarding any seeds as you go. Layer these slices with the sugar in a small bowl, scraping any juice over them that may have been squeezed out during slicing. Cover with plastic wrap and allow to stand, unrefrigerated, until the next day.

When ready to assemble pie, preheat the oven to 375 degrees.

Using a slotted spoon, remove the lemon slices from the liquid and spread over the cooked crust (which is still in its pan). Beat the eggs and mix with the lemon liquid and lemon rind. Pour over lemon slices. Bake for 25 to 30 minutes, until puffy.

Serve this with a little sweetened cream if you like.
Serves 6 to 8

LEE KLEIN'S PIE CRUST

- 1¼ cups all-purpose flour
- 1 tablespoon sugar (optional)
- ½ teaspoon salt
- 6 tablespoons frozen butter
- 4 tablespoons frozen vegetable shortening
- 3 tablespoons ice water

Preheat the oven to 425 degrees.

Mix the flour, sugar, and salt in a food processor. Pulse just a couple of times. Add the butter and vegetable shortening. Add water and pulse a few more times. Gather into a ball. There should be bits of butter showing in the dough. Form into a ball, flatten it, and wrap in waxed paper. Refrigerate for 30 minutes.

Roll pastry out on a floured surface and line an 8-inch pan. Prick bottom with tines of a fork. Cover with a piece of foil and weight with dried beans. Bake until set, about 5 minutes. Remove foil and beans and continue baking until the pastry is beginning to turn golden, pricking any blisters which may form on the bottom of the crust, about 10 or more minutes. This should not completely bake, since it will have to be cooked again when the filling is added.
Makes 1 single 8-inch crust

CHICKEN BREASTS BAKED IN RED BELL PEPPERS

Here is a French method of cooking chicken that a friend told me about.

6   large red bell peppers
¼   cup olive oil
3   small chicken breasts, boned, about 1½ pounds
    Salt and black pepper to taste
2   garlic cloves, cut into 6 slivers each
2   tablespoons chopped fresh tarragon
4   slices thick bacon, fried well and drained
2   tablespoons cold unsalted butter, cut into 6 pieces
6   tablespoons chicken stock

Cut the stems out of the peppers and remove the seeds and ribs, leaving peppers whole. Rub inside of each pepper well with some of the oil. Set aside.

Preheat the oven to 375 degrees.

Cut each chicken breast in half lengthwise and rub well with the balance of the oil. Lay halves out and pound very lightly. Salt and pepper well. Distribute the garlic and tarragon over

the breasts. Cut bacon into small pieces and also distribute among breasts. Place one of the pieces of cold butter in the middle of each chicken breast.

Fold chicken over and fit into the peppers. Drizzle the oil, if any, into the peppers. Put a tablespoon of stock in each and carefully place peppers on their sides in an ovenproof pan into which they fit snugly. Place in the oven and lay a sheet of foil loosely on the top. Bake about 40 minutes, basting once. Remove foil and bake another 15 to 20 minutes. If there is no pan juice for basting, use a little stock.
Serves 6

SWEET POTATO PANCAKES

Since I love sweet potatoes, this is a variation I'm particularly partial to.

- 4 **cups shredded sweet potatoes**
- 1 **medium onion, grated**
- 1 **teaspoon salt**
  Scant ½ teaspoon black pepper
- 3 **tablespoons flour**
- 2 **large eggs**
- 3 **tablespoons unsalted butter**
- 3 **tablespoons safflower oil**

Place shredded potatoes and onion in a small bowl and toss. Add salt and pepper and toss again. Sprinkle flour over all and mix. Stir in the eggs.

Heat butter and oil in a large skillet over medium heat. When hot, divide potato mixture into 12 portions and slide each carefully into hot fat. Flatten slightly with a pancake turner and cook until lightly golden without turning, 3 minutes or less. Turn and cook other side, flattening again slightly, until golden, about 2 minutes.

Drain on paper towels.
Makes 12 pancakes

LEFT: *Indian summer.* ABOVE: *Chicken Breasts Baked in Red Bell Peppers.* RIGHT: *Mesclun Salad.*

MESCLUN SALAD WITH CHEVRE VINAIGRETTE

If you can't find mesclun, use any combination of greens you like, just as long as you have a good mixture of textures and flavors.

- 8 **cups loosely packed mesclun, well washed and dried**
- 2 **tablespoons cider vinegar**
- 6 **tablespoons vegetable oil**
- 2 **ounces creamy chèvre (goat) cheese**
  Salt and black pepper to taste

Place mesclun in a large salad bowl and refrigerate, covered.

Whisk together the vinegar and oil. Whisk in chèvre until well combined. Add salt and pepper. Pour over greens.
Serves 6

WHITE CHOCOLATE
ICE CREAM

Here is yet another recipe devised by the multitalented food writer and consultant Lee Klein.

1   pint half-and-half
⅓   cup superfine sugar
    Salt
4   large egg yolks
1½ teaspoons vanilla extract
4   ounces white chocolate
6   tablespoons buttermilk
2   teaspoons fresh lemon juice

Put half-and-half in a small saucepan and bring to a boil. Transfer to the top of a double boiler and stir in sugar and a pinch of salt. Beat egg yolks. With half-and-half mixture set over boiling water, add a little of the half-and-half to the yolks to warm them, then pour the yolks into the half-and-half in a thin stream, stirring. Continue cooking over boiling water, stirring, until mixture coats a spoon, several minutes. Strain and stir in vanilla. Set aside off the heat.

Break the white chocolate into small pieces and place in a small pan with a tablespoon or so of milk or cream. Melt the white chocolate over low heat and immediately stir into the half-and-half mixture, rinsing out the chocolate pan with the cream. Set aside to cool.

When cool, stir in the buttermilk and lemon juice. Refrigerate, covered, until cold. Pour into a commercial ice-cream maker and freeze according to manufacturer's instructions.

Serve with berries, if desired.
Makes about 1½ pints

ABOVE: *White Chocolate Ice Cream.*
LEFT: *The last of the hollyhocks.*
RIGHT: *A quiet inlet.*

PIMIENTO CHICKEN WITH
MUSHROOMS ON BUTTERMILK–
SOUR CREAM CORN BREAD

GREEN SALAD WITH ANCHOVY
VINAIGRETTE

COEUR A LA CREME

PIMIENTO CHICKEN WITH MUSHROOMS ON BUTTERMILK–SOUR CREAM CORN BREAD

This recipe makes plenty of sauce to be absorbed by the corn bread. Be generous when you serve it.

5 small boneless chicken breasts, skinned (about 2¼ pounds, boned weight)
  Salt and black pepper to taste
6 tablespoons unsalted butter
6 tablespoons margarine
2 tablespoons corn oil
1¼ cups coarsely chopped onions
4 tablespoons flour
4 cups chicken stock, heated
¼ cup minced shallots
12 ounces fresh mushrooms, thickly sliced

1 7-ounce jar pimientos, drained and cut into large dice
1 cup low-fat sour cream
2 tablespoons minced fresh parsley
  Buttermilk–Sour Cream Corn Bread (page 129)
  Watercress for garnish (optional)

Split each chicken breast and cut the halves in two crosswise. Salt, then pepper very generously. Place 5 tablespoons each of the butter and margarine in a Dutch oven along with the oil. Heat. When bubbly, lightly brown chicken pieces in batches, cooking over high heat for 2 minutes per side. As pieces are finished, drain on paper towels. Pour out most of oil mixture, leaving about 6 tablespoons.

Add onions to pot and brown them over high heat, about 1 minutes, stirring constantly to keep from burning. Sprinkle flour over all and continue to cook for another minute or so, stirring with a flat-ended pancake turner, scraping the bottom as you go. This mixture will start to brown and when it does, quickly add hot stock. Mix well to deglaze pot and simmer for a minute to thicken, then add reserved chicken. Cover and simmer over very low heat

for 1 hour or slightly more. You may allow this to cool and refrigerate it at this point.

To complete the dish, place the balance of the butter and margarine in a medium skillet and add the shallots. Toss over medium heat for about 30 seconds to wilt, then add mushrooms. Sauté for another minute or so, then cover and continue to cook, shaking pan occasionally, until the mushrooms are almost wilted and have given up some juice, about 2 minutes. Add to the chicken, along with the pimientos. Mix carefully and simmer briefly. Stir in the sour cream and parsley. Cook another few minutes over low heat, to be sure the flavors are blended and the chicken is hot.

To serve, place split (and buttered if you like) squares of hot corn bread on individual plates and spoon chicken and a generous amount of sauce over all. Garnish with watercress.
Serves 6, generously

ABOVE: *Dinner in front of the fire.*
OPPOSITE TOP: *Pimiento Chicken with Mushrooms.* OPPOSITE BOTTOM: *Green Salad with Anchovy Vinaigrette.*

BUTTERMILK–SOUR CREAM CORN BREAD

This corn bread does occasionally stick to the bottom of the pan, even when the pan has been sprayed. You might want to line the bottom of the pan with waxed paper to be on the safe side.

2 cups white cornmeal
3½ teaspoons baking powder
½ teaspoon baking soda
1½ teaspoons salt
1½ cups low-fat sour cream
2 large eggs, lightly beaten
2 tablespoons corn oil
⅔ cup buttermilk

Preheat the oven to 425 degrees. Coat well an 8x11-inch pan with vegetable-oil spray and set aside or spray and line bottom with waxed paper.

Sift together the dry ingredients. Set aside. Lightly beat together the sour cream, eggs, and oil. Mix quickly with the dry ingredients (do not overmix) and pour into pan. Pour buttermilk over the top of the batter.

Bake for 30 to 35 minutes or until lightly browned. Cut into 12 pieces.
Makes 12 servings

GREEN SALAD WITH ANCHOVY VINAIGRETTE

Anchovy vinaigrette is also very good on fresh tomatoes. And chèvre spread on slices of baguette is a fine accompaniment.

6 cups carefully washed and dried Boston lettuce, or other greens, torn into large pieces
48 sugar snap peas, blanched 1 minute in boiling water
2 tablespoons red wine vinegar
1 generous teaspoon grainy Dijon-style mustard

2 tablespoons olive oil
3 tablespoons safflower oil
Black pepper to taste
4 flat anchovy filets, drained and mashed

Place the lettuce and sugar snaps in a large salad bowl and refrigerate, covered, until ready to use.

Whisk together the vinegar, mustard, oils, and pepper. Stir in the anchovies and mix until they "dissolve."

Toss with the greens and sugar snaps.
Serves 6

———

COEUR A LA CREME

This very simple recipe produces delicious results.

8 ounces cream cheese
¾ cup sifted confectioners' sugar
1 teaspoon lemon juice
1 teaspoon grated lemon rind
1 teaspoon vanilla extract
1 tablespoon framboise *eau-de-vie*
1¼ cups heavy cream, whipped to soft peaks

Combine the cream cheese and sugar. Beat together until smooth. Beat in lemon juice, lemon rind, vanilla, and framboise. Mix well. Fold in the whipped cream.

Line a *coeur à la crème* mold or a small loosely woven basket with a double layer of cheesecloth. Pour mixture in and smooth the top. Cover with cheesecloth and place on a plate. Put in the refrigerator overnight to "weep." Discard any liquid from the plate.

Invert onto a serving dish, remove cheesecloth, and serve with seasonal fruit tossed with a little lemon juice and sugar to taste.
Serves 6 to 8

Coeur à la Crème.

Two Fish Dinners

ALTHOUGH I LIKED FISH, usually fried, when I was a kid, it really wasn't until my days in Bridgehampton that I truly discovered how delicious it could be. Until then I hadn't even bothered to investigate its variety of flavors. However, I think the most important thing I came to realize was that the simpler its preparation, the better. Grilled, broiled, or baked without elaborate stuffings is the ticket.

Here are two of my favorites.

SALT-COOKED SALMON FILETS WITH DILL
AND SHALLOT BUTTER

CHEVRE MASHED POTATOES

SAUTEED CHERRY TOMATOES

MERINGUE TART

SALT-COOKED SALMON FILETS WITH DILL AND SHALLOT BUTTER

The only drawback to this way of cooking is that it creates smoke. You can minimize this by putting your skillets as directly under your exhaust fan as possible. And when you cover the pans with foil, press down lightly around three sides, leaving the fourth (open side) acting as a sort of chimney that you can direct toward the back of your stove and toward the exhaust fan.

Now, you can get similar results by preparing this in the oven. To do so, preheat the oven to 450 degrees. Place the salted skillets in the oven and preheat them for 15 minutes. Place fish filets in pans and follow the recipe, leaving the oven at 450 degrees, as for cooking on top of the stove.

That said, I still think the taste is better when you cook them on the stove — smoke and all.

2 tablespoons unsalted butter, softened
2 tablespoons minced shallots
  Coarse salt
4 thick salmon filets with skin on, about 2 pounds
3 tablespoons coarsely chopped fresh dill (no stems)
  Fresh lemon juice to taste

Mash together the butter and shallots. Set aside. Put a generous layer of coarse salt in the bottom of 2 iron skillets, each large enough to hold 2 filets comfortably. Put over high heat until very hot. Add filets, skin side down, and cook for 1 minute. Spread the softened shallot butter on each of the filets, sprinkle with the dill, then add a squeeze of lemon. Cook for another minute.

Cover the pans lightly with foil and then turn the heat back to medium-low. Cook for an additional 6 minutes or slightly more, until flaky but moist. Do not overcook.
Serves 4

Summer dinner.

CHEVRE MASHED POTATOES

This dish has a very subtle flavor.

- 2 pounds large red potatoes, peeled and cut into large cubes
- 3 tablespoons unsalted butter
- ½ cup half-and-half
- 7 ounces creamy chèvre (goat) cheese
- 2 teaspoons salt
- ¾ teaspoon white pepper

Cover the potatoes with cold water. Bring to a boil and cook until fork-tender, about 12 minutes.

Meanwhile heat together the butter, half-and-half, and chèvre. Stir until chèvre melts. Set aside.

Drain the potatoes and dump back into the pot. Cover with a tea towel and shake pan over medium heat for about 30 seconds to dry out.

Pour in chèvre mixture and mash with a hand masher until smooth, adding salt and pepper along the way.

Add more warm half-and-half or milk if you want these to be less thick.
Serves 6

SAUTEED CHERRY TOMATOES

Mix whatever cherry tomatoes you find in your market. If you see nothing but red, they will be fine alone.

- 2 tablespoons unsalted butter
- 1 pint yellow pear tomatoes, washed, dried, and cut in half
- 1 pint red or orange cherry tomatoes, washed, dried, and cut in half
- ¼ cup minced fresh parsley
- ½ teaspoon salt, or to taste
- ¼ teaspoon black pepper

Melt the butter over medium heat in a large skillet. Add the tomatoes and toss. Sprinkle parsley, salt, and pepper over all and continue to cook, tossing lightly, until warmed through and skins are beginning to brown, several minutes.
Serves 6

———

MERINGUE TART

This is a version of a very old dessert.

- ½ cup granulated sugar
- ½ cup confectioners' sugar
- 3 large egg whites
- 1½ cups heavy cream
- 1 teaspoon vanilla extract
- 1 cup chopped pecans or walnuts, well toasted
- ¼ ounce or more semisweet chocolate, grated

Preheat the oven to 300 degrees.

Mix the sugars in a bowl and add the egg whites. Beat with a hand mixer at a slow speed until frothy, then beat at high speed until whites stand in stiff peaks. This will take 7 minutes or more. Coat a 9-inch pie pan with vegetable-oil spray. Add meringue and smooth top. Bake for 1 hour or until golden.

Allow to cool. Whip the cream to soft peaks and fold in the vanilla and nuts. Crush top of meringue in the center (if it has not already settled) and heap on the cream, smoothing top. Decorate with grated chocolate.

Refrigerate for 1 hour. Loosen edges before serving.
Serves 6

LEFT: *Salt-Cooked Salmon Filets, Chèvre Mashed Potatoes, and Sautéed Cherry Tomatoes.* BELOW: *Meringue Tart.*

BROILED FLUKE WITH ONION–HOT PEPPER TOPPING

If fluke isn't available, substitute any mild white fish. The oil in the pan is to keep the fish from sticking or burning on top, and the soy sauce should coat the filets evenly on both sides. The quantity of herbs may be varied to suit your taste. Same with the butter. I don't use any salt because there's enough in the soy sauce.

2 tablespoons safflower oil
6 fluke filets, about 1¾ pounds
¼ cup light soy sauce
¼ cup coarsely chopped green onions, with some green
1½ tablespoons coarsely chopped fresh Italian parsley
1½ tablespoons coarsely chopped fresh dill
Juice of ½ large lemon, plus wedges for garnish
3 tablespoons unsalted butter
Black pepper to taste
Onion–Hot Pepper Topping (recipe follows)

Preheat the broiler and place the tray on the lowest rung.

Line a shallow pan large enough to hold the 6 filets in one layer with foil. Spread oil evenly in the pan, then add the filets, turning and coating both sides. Rub both sides with soy sauce. Arrange fish skin side down. Sprinkle with the green onions, parsley, and dill. (It's better to have too much of this herb mixture than too little.) Squeeze the lemon over all. Dot with butter and add pepper to taste.

Broil without turning until fish just flakes, 3 to 5 minutes depending on its thickness. The herbs may blacken slightly in spots, but that is all right. Lift directly onto the individual warmed dinner plates with a spatula. Garnish with lemon wedges and serve with Onion–Hot Pepper Topping.
Serves 6

ONION–HOT PEPPER TOPPING

I use the long red, semihot Mexican peppers here. If you have the strength for them, you may use the hotter ones. But if you do, warn your guests.

5 tablespoons olive oil
3 large red onions, very thinly sliced
3 long red, medium-hot peppers, cut in half lengthwise, seeded and cut into ½-inch pieces
½ to ¾ teaspoon salt
¾ teaspoon sugar
5 teaspoons red wine vinegar

In a large skillet over medium heat, warm half the olive oil. Toss in onions and peppers to coat. Turn heat to low and wilt the onions, being careful not to burn them. After about 6 minutes, add the balance of the olive oil, salt, and sugar. Cook several more minutes, stirring occasionally to keep from burning. When onions have started turning dark, about 10 minutes, sprinkle with the vinegar and cook 2 minutes more.

———

RICE AND PEANUT PILAF

I've got to confess — I like peanuts in almost anything.

4 tablespoons (½ stick) unsalted butter
¾ cup minced onion
1 cup long-grain rice, washed
2 cups hot chicken stock
¾ cup toasted, lightly salted peanuts

Preheat the oven to 375 degrees.

Melt the butter in a small pot over medium heat and add the onion. Sauté until wilted, about 5 minutes. Mix in the rice and stir in the hot stock and peanuts. Bring quickly back to a boil.

Cover, reduce heat to low, and bake until rice is tender, 20 to 25 minutes. Fluff rice before serving.
Serves 6

———

WARM GREEN BEAN SALAD

I'm very fond of this salad because it's so flexible. You may serve the beans tossed with hot vinaigrette at the last minute, but you may also add any number of ingredients, either tossed in with them or as a garnish. Consider minced red onion, celery, red bell pepper, shallots, parsley, or dill. Or what about a topping of toasted slivered almonds, pimiento, crumbled crisp bacon, or chopped hard-cooked egg?

Anyway, here is the basic "recipe."

1 teaspoon salt, or to taste
1 generous teaspoon Dijon-style mustard
Scant ½ teaspoon black pepper
2 tablespoons balsamic vinegar
5 tablespoons olive oil
1¼ pounds small string beans, tipped, stemmed, and steamed to crisp-tender

Whisk together the salt, mustard, pepper, and vinegar. Whisk in the oil. Heat the vinaigrette in a small saucepan and toss with the freshly steamed beans. Combine or garnish with any of the ingredients suggested above.
Serves 6

———

BROWN SUGAR PIE WITH BERRY SAUCE

This recipe provides you with enough crust for two pies, so freeze half. The filling reduces a lot while it cooks — but what's left is delicious.

PASTRY

¾	cup vegetable shortening
¼	cup boiling water
1	tablespoon half-and-half or milk
2	cups all-purpose flour
1	teaspoon salt
1	tablespoon superfine sugar

FILLING

2	cups heavy cream
4	tablespoons granulated sugar
4	tablespoons Brownulated sugar
1	tablespoon unsalted butter

Make the pastry: Place the shortening in a bowl and pour boiling water over it. Beat to combine. Stir in half-and-half and set aside.

Place the flour, salt, and superfine sugar in a food processor, whirl a couple of times to mix, and spoon the shortening mixture in. Process until mixture forms a ball, only about 30 seconds. Remove dough, which will be very damp, divide in half, and place each half on a sheet of waxed paper. Cover with another sheet and press the dough into a 7-inch circle. Fold edges of paper to close and refrigerate one portion for at least 1 hour before using. Freeze the other half.

Complete the pie: Preheat the oven to 400 degrees.

Mix the cream and granulated sugar in a medium pot and bring to a boil. Whisk down and let it boil up again. Whisk down. Turn heat to barely a simmer and allow to cook for 20 minutes, whisking once or twice.

Meanwhile, roll out the dough slightly thicker than for an ordinary pie, about ³/₁₆ inch, and line a 9-inch pie pan, being careful not to leave any holes for the filling to seep through. (The filling will burn during cooking if it gets under the crust.) Fold under the edges and crimp decoratively. Sprinkle the Brownulated sugar over the bottom.

Mix the butter into the thickened cream and pour it into the pan. Bake for 30 to 40 minutes or until top is getting golden in patches and the filling jiggles slightly when shaken.

ABOVE: *Broiled Fluke, Rice and Peanut Pilaf, and Warm Green Bean Salad.* OVERLEAF: *Brown Sugar Pie with Berry Sauce.*

Allow to cool several hours to set. Serve as is or on a slick of Berry Sauce (recipe follows) or with fresh fruit slices and their juice.
Serves 6 to 8

BERRY SAUCE

1	pint fresh berries
¾	cup sugar or to taste
1	teaspoon fresh lemon juice

Combine all ingredients in a nonreactive saucepan and bring slowly to a boil over medium heat, stirring. Remove from heat and put through a fine sieve. Discard seeds and pulp. Refrigerate before using.
Makes 1½ cups

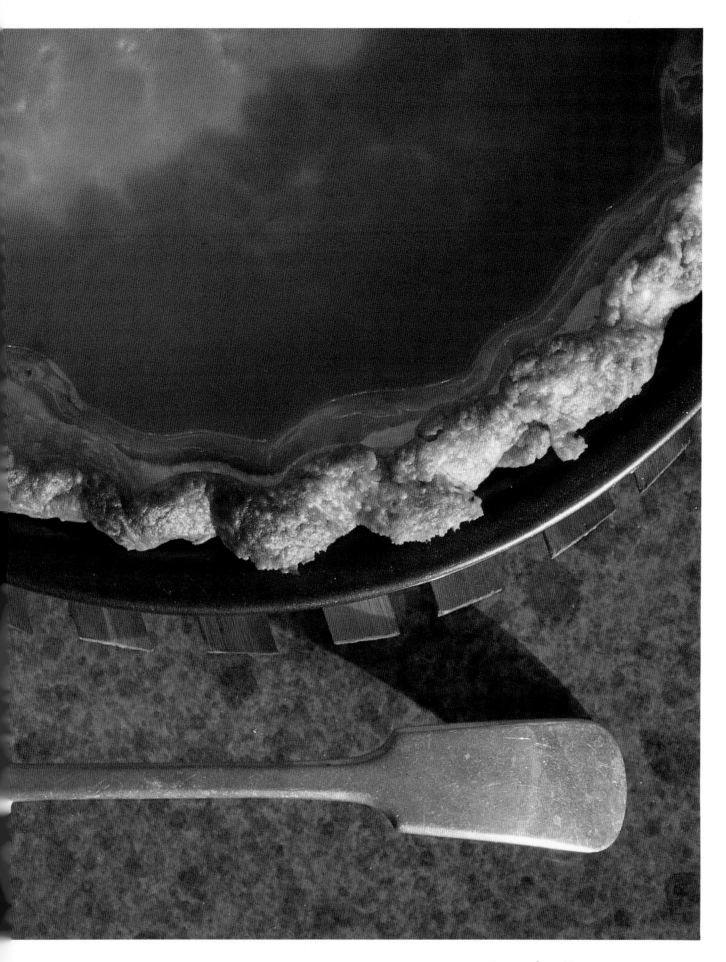

In
New York City

Roasted Tenderloin Variations

WHEN I FIRST STARTED cooking at home for friends, I quickly realized, as I've said often before, that I didn't want to spend all my time in the kitchen while my guests were whooping it up in the living room. So along the way I started collecting recipes and devising menus that could pretty much be prepared in advance and then put together in the last thirty minutes before the guests were called to table. This has worked well over the years, but obviously it limited what I could cook and still be free for time with my friends.

Of course, if I were the sort who likes to have everyone crowding around in the kitchen while I am cooking the problem probably never would've come up in the first place. But I'm not like that. Cooking is one thing, socializing is another, and in my case the twain might bend, but they don't ever really meet.

Maybe it's the changing times or simply needing change for its own sake, but lately I've noticed I've wanted to try new things, things I couldn't do with my self-imposed restrictions. Where I used to be content to have a stew, a hearty soup, or a quickly prepared fish as the main attraction, there were those occasions when I've wished for a way of doing a roast that didn't leave me nervously timing it and then grappling with carving — or for that matter, to do things that were simply lighter.

OPPOSITE: *At the Greenmarket.*
ABOVE: *Table set under the mural.*

Of course, when I've had a good kitchen helper, I've prepared more complicated meals, but such help wasn't always at my side. Also, there have been other occasions when I've just wanted to *try* more complex dishes. But you can bet almost none of these found its way into my regular repertoire if it involved too many steps or was in the least bit temperamental.

Anyway, this is just a stretched-out way to introduce you to a method of preparing meat — seared and briefly roasted — that seems to have several tremendous advantages. Tenderloins of beef, pork, lamb, veal, venison, and antelope are all delicious when cooked in this manner. Quick and easy to prepare and serve, they are also lower in fat and cholesterol. When accompanied by a do-ahead vegetable, sauce, and garnish, followed by salad with cheese and dessert, you can make imaginative (and elegant) menus with a minimum of fuss. The only disadvantage is that these are all expensive cuts of meat. But when you compare the cost of a dinner for six at home using even this costly ingredient with the same at a quality restaurant, you are still way ahead of the game.

Incidentally, I'm sure that you, like many of us, often on impulse buy or are given relishes, chutneys, and pickled or preserved vegetables and fruit, which then sit on your pantry shelves for ages. I usually forget that I have them. Well, these menus are a perfect place to use such delicious oddments.

ROAST TENDERLOIN OF BEEF
WITH SHALLOT BUTTER

GREEN CHILI SPOONBREAD

CORNICHONS AND OLIVES

ROAST TENDERLOIN OF BEEF WITH SHALLOT BUTTER

This cut of beef is also called prime filet mignon or filet of beef. It is always served either rare or medium-rare, never well done. Be sure meat is at almost room temperature when you start.

2½ pounds tenderloin of beef
2 teaspoons soy sauce
4 teaspoons black pepper
2 tablespoons olive oil
3 tablespoons unsalted butter, softened
2 tablespoons minced shallots

Preheat the oven to 450 degrees.

Cut the tenderloin across into 2 pieces. Rub with the soy sauce and press the black pepper into all sides. Heat oil in a heavy skillet over high heat. Sear meat on all sides, about 3 minutes. Roast for 18 to 20 minutes, turning meat once halfway through the cooking time for medium-rare. Test it after 18 minutes, as this timing can vary by several minutes depending on the thickness of the meat. The internal temperature should be about 120 degrees.

Mash the butter and shallots together. Put a dab on each serving.
Serves 6

GREEN CHILI SPOONBREAD

This is the simplest spoonbread recipe I know of, and it's one of the best.

2 cups milk
2 large eggs
2 tablespoons unsalted butter
⅔ cup white cornmeal
1 teaspoon salt
2 teaspoons sugar (optional)

ABOVE: *The Beef with Shallot Butter menu.* OPPOSITE: *The Veal with Natural Sauce menu.*

1 4-ounce can mild green chilies, drained and minced
2 teaspoons baking powder

Preheat the oven to 450 degrees and generously butter a 1½-quart soufflé dish. Combine ⅔ cup of milk with the eggs and beat well. Set aside.

In a medium saucepan over low heat, combine remaining milk with the butter and bring just to a simmer. Increase heat slightly and add the cornmeal in a steady stream, stirring constantly. Stir in salt. Remove from heat and pour in milk-egg mixture. Whisk until smooth. Add chilies and whisk to combine. Sprinkle baking powder over all and continue whisking to combine.

Pour batter into soufflé dish and bake until puffy and golden, about 30 minutes.

Serve immediately.
Serves 6 to 8

ROAST TENDERLOIN OF VEAL WITH NATURAL SAUCE

This meat has a very gentle flavor. I like it with a hint of tarragon. The veal should be at room temperature when you start to cook it.

2½ pounds veal tenderloin
    Salt and white pepper to taste
1   small onion, thinly sliced
1   small carrot, thinly sliced
1   teaspoon dried tarragon
2   cups veal or chicken stock
2   tablespoons plus 1 teaspoon
    unsalted butter, softened
1   tablespoon vegetable oil
1   teaspoon flour

Preheat the oven to 450 degrees.

Salt and pepper the pieces of veal. Set aside. Meanwhile, combine the vegetables and chicken stock. Bring to a boil, then simmer over medium-low heat for about 8 minutes. Set aside.

Place 2 tablespoons of the butter and the vegetable oil in a heavy skillet and sear veal over high heat until browned on all sides, about 2 minutes. Place in the oven and roast 7 to 9 minutes, turning once, until light pink inside. Test for doneness after 8 minutes.

Remove to a cutting board and cover lightly with foil.

Strain stock and discard vegetables. Pour out any fat and deglaze pan with liquid. Mash flour and remaining teaspoon of butter together and stir into sauce. Simmer for several minutes.

Serve veal slices with a few spoons of the sauce over each.
Serves 6

LETTUCE PROSCIUTTO RISOTTO

This is based on Barbara Kafka's wonderful recipe.

2   tablespoons unsalted butter
2   tablespoons olive oil
½   cup minced onion
1   cup Arborio rice
3¼ cups chicken stock, heated
1   cup shredded lettuce
1   cup shredded prosciutto,
    about 4 ounces
    Black pepper to taste

Place the butter and oil in a 14x11x2-inch dish and cook 2 minutes on high, uncovered, in a microwave oven. Stir in onion and cook 2 minutes. Stir in rice and cook another 2 minutes. Pour in heated stock and cook 9 minutes. Stir in lettuce and prosciutto and cook 9 minutes more. Allow to rest for several minutes before serving, topped with a grind of fresh pepper.
Serves 6

ROAST TENDERLOIN OF LAMB WITH WINE SAUCE

Here's an exception. Tenderloin of lamb is so small that what I use is really a boned rack of lamb.

Almost all wine reduction sauces are basically the same idea — made from wine reduced with mirepoix (a classic combination of the vegetables and herbs you see below) and further reduced with the addition of stock. They vary only in the proportion of the ingredients to one another.

WINE SAUCE

- 1¼ cups dry red wine
- 1 small onion, thickly sliced
- 1 small carrot, scraped and thickly sliced
- ½ bay leaf
- 2 sprigs parsley
- 1 cup veal or chicken stock
- 1 teaspoon tomato paste

ROAST

- 3 boned racks of lamb, fat trimmed off, about 10 ounces each
- Salt, black pepper, and dried rosemary to taste
- 3 tablespoons unsalted butter

Make the wine sauce: Place the wine, onion, carrot, bay leaf, and parsley in a small nonreactive pot. Boil rapidly until reduced to 4 or 5 tablespoons, about 6 to 8 minutes. Meanwhile, reduce stock to 3 or 4 tablespoons, about 6 minutes. Strain vegetables out of wine and discard. Combine the wine and stock and stir in the tomato paste. Simmer for a minute, then set aside.

Prepare the roast: Preheat the oven to 450 degrees.

Sprinkle the lamb lightly with salt and generously with pepper, pressing it in place. Press in the rosemary.

Melt 2 tablespoons of the butter over medium-high heat in a heavy skillet large enough to hold the 3 pieces of lamb comfortably. When butter is just starting to turn golden, add the lamb and sear on all sides, 2 to 3 minutes.

Place the skillet in the oven and bake for 7 to 10 minutes. About 9 minutes usually produces pink lamb, but this will depend on the thickness of the lamb. Cut into the middle after 9 minutes and take a peek.

Remove lamb to a cutting board and allow to rest a few minutes before slicing, loosely covered with foil.

While lamb is resting, pour out any fat from the skillet and pour in the wine sauce. Deglaze the pan. Whisk in the balance of the butter.

Serve with a few spoons of the heated sauce over each serving.

Serves 6

———

WARM WHITE BEANS WITH RED ONION CHUTNEY

You can use any method of cooking the white beans you like, but here is how I do it: soak a 1-pound package of white beans overnight. Drain them and put into a pot with 8 cups of chicken stock, 1 large bay leaf, and ½ teaspoon of thyme. Simmer until tender, about 1½ hours. Cool and refrigerate, undrained. Leftovers are good in soup.

- 2 cups cooked white beans, drained
- 6 tablespoons chopped red onion
- 3 tablespoons olive oil
- 1 tablespoon raspberry vinegar
- 2 garlic cloves, roasted (optional)
- Black pepper to taste

Toss the beans and onion together. Whisk together the olive oil, vinegar, and squeezed-out pulp of the garlic. Pour over beans and mix in a generous grinding of black pepper.

Serves 4 to 6

ROAST TENDERLOIN OF PORK WITH MUSTARD WINE SAUCE

As you probably know already, pork may be served slightly pink, which makes it less dry. Start out with the meat at room temperature.

- 2½ pounds tenderloin of pork
- Salt to taste
- 2 teaspoons black pepper
- 1 teaspoon dried thyme
- 2 tablespoons olive oil
- 1 medium garlic clove, minced
- 3 medium shallots, minced
- ⅓ cup dry red wine
- 1½ tablespoons Dijon-style mustard
- 1 cup beef stock
- 5 tablespoons heavy cream
- 2 tablespoons unsalted butter

Preheat the oven to 450 degrees.

Sprinkle the pork with salt and press in the pepper and thyme. Place oil in a heavy skillet and sear meat over high heat for about 3 minutes, browning all sides. Place in the oven and roast, turning once, until the internal temperature is 160 degrees, about 16 minutes.

When the meat is done, remove to a cutting board and cover lightly with foil. Pour fat from the skillet and add the garlic and shallots and cook for several minutes over medium-low heat until lightly brown. Add the wine and increase the heat to high; simmer for 1 minute. Stir in mustard, stock, and cream and bring to a boil. Reduce heat and simmer until reduced to 1 cup, about 6 minutes. Reduce heat to low and stir in butter.

Top each serving with a few teaspoons of the sauce.

Serves 6

ABOVE: *The Lamb with Wine Sauce menu.* BELOW: *The Pork with Mustard Wine Sauce menu.*

ABOVE: *The Venison with Cabernet Sauce menu.* BELOW: *Produce at Union Square.*

ROASTED PEPPER SALAD

I use several colors of peppers for this, but you could use all of one variety.

- 1 *each* red, yellow, orange, and purple sweet bell pepper, roasted and peeled
- 2 tablespoons minced shallots
- ½ cup olive oil
- ⅓ cup dry white wine
- ½ cup white wine vinegar
- 1 teaspoon dried oregano
- 1 tablespoon sugar
- ½ teaspoon cayenne pepper

Cut each pepper into strips and place in a shallow dish. Combine all other ingredients in a small saucepan and bring to a simmer. Pour over peppers. Allow to cool and refrigerate. Bring back to room temperature before serving.
Serves 8 or more

SWEET POTATO AND GRAPEFRUIT CASSEROLE

Yams, sweet potatoes . . . I love them whatever they're called.

- 4 medium to small sweet potatoes, about 1½ pounds
- 1 large grapefruit
- 3 tablespoons unsalted butter
- ¼ cup plus 1 tablespoon light brown sugar, tightly packed
  Pinch of salt
- 2 large eggs, well beaten

Preheat the oven to 375 degrees.

Place the potatoes, unpeeled, in a large saucepan and cover with water. Peel the grapefruit and put the rind in with the potatoes. Bring to a boil and simmer until potatoes are just fork-tender, about 20 minutes.

Meanwhile, dip the peeled grapefruit into a pan of hot water, turning constantly for approximately 30 seconds. Remove the pulp from the sections over a bowl to catch the juice. Discard the white skin.

When the potatoes are done, drain, discarding the rind. Peel the potatoes and put into a food processor along with the grapefruit pulp and juice, butter, brown sugar, and salt. Puree and then taste to check sweetness. If grapefruit is not very sweet, you might want to add more sugar. Stir in eggs.

Pour into a well-buttered, 6-cup soufflé dish. Place in a pan of hot water and bake for approximately 45 minutes, until center is set.
Serves 8

ROAST TENDERLOIN OF VENISON
WITH CABERNET SAUCE

CABBAGE, POTATO, SWEET
PEPPER, AND ONION MÉLANGE

ROAST TENDERLOIN OF VENISON WITH CABERNET SAUCE

This red meat has as few calories and cholesterol as chicken.

- 2½ pounds tenderloin of axis venison, or Denver cut (see *Note*)
- 2 large garlic cloves, minced
  Salt and black pepper to taste
- 2 tablespoons olive oil
- 1½ cups Cabernet Sauvignon
- ½ cup coarsely chopped shallots
- 1 small carrot, thinly sliced
- 1 bay leaf
- 2 sprigs parsley
- 1 cup beef broth
- 1 tablespoon cold unsalted butter

Preheat the oven to 450 degrees.

Rub the venison with garlic and sprinkle with salt and pepper. Put olive oil in a heavy skillet. Add venison and sear over high heat until browned on all sides, about 3 minutes. Place in oven and roast for about 16 minutes, turning once, until medium-rare.

Meanwhile, combine the wine with the vegetables and herbs and bring to a boil. Reduce by half over medium heat, about 8 minutes. Strain out vegetables and discard. In a saucepan reduce broth by half, about 7 minutes over high heat. Combine the liquids.

When meat is done, remove to cutting board and cover loosely with foil. Pour any fat from the pan and deglaze with the reduced liquids. Whisk in the cold butter and add salt and pepper.

Spoon a bit of the sauce over each serving of meat.
Serves 6

Note: Venison is becoming available in more and more markets. But if you can't find it near you, order it from the Texas Wild Game Cooperative at (800) 962-4263.

CABBAGE, POTATO, SWEET PEPPER, AND ONION MELANGE

I love this combination of vegetables. It's something my housekeeper Grace Monroe taught me to cook.

- 1 strip thick bacon, cut into 6 pieces
- 1 tablespoon unsalted butter
- 1 large potato, sliced
- ¾ pound green cabbage, shredded
- ½ *each* red and yellow bell pepper, seeded and cut into strips
- 1 large onion, sliced thick
- 2 tablespoons water
- ½ teaspoon salt
- ½ teaspoon black pepper

Fry the bacon pieces in a medium to large saucepan over medium heat until half-crisp. Pour out fat. Continue frying until crisp. Add butter and melt. Add potato. Rinse cabbage with cold water and add to saucepan with whatever water is clinging to it. Add peppers and onion. Sprinkle the water over all. Season with salt and pepper.

Cover tightly and simmer or steam for 10 minutes. Toss and continue cooking, tossing once more to mix until potato is cooked, about 30 minutes in all. Do not overcook.
Serves 6 to 8

Five Simple Salads

CHEVRE-STUFFED
ENDIVE SPEARS

You may serve a plate of these stuffed Belgian endive spears or serve them surrounding a mound of dressed salad greens. Use a teaspoon of soft mild chèvre (goat) cheese to stuff each spear, and when they are arranged on individual plates (with the salad greens), top the whole thing with a good grind of black pepper.

———

ENDIVE AND RADICCHIO
WITH WHITE CHEDDAR
CHEESE

To make this salad, toss together torn leaves of radicchio and cut or broken pieces of Belgian endive. Make a dressing with olive oil and balsamic vinegar, using equal amounts of each with 1 extra tablespoon of oil. Toss and season with salt and pepper. Serve with a piece of good white cheddar.

———

MIXED GREEN SALAD
WITH ASIAGO CHEESE

Toss together any mixture of well-washed greens you like and dress with the following vinaigrette. Serve with a piece of aged Asiago cheese.

- 2 teaspoons Dijon-style mustard
- 2 tablespoons red wine vinegar
- ½ teaspoon salt
- ¼ teaspoon black pepper
- ¼ cup olive oil

Whisk together all ingredients.
Makes a scant ½ cup, enough vinaigrette for about 6 servings

BOSTON LETTUCE SALAD
WITH WALNUT
VINAIGRETTE AND
CAMBAZOLA CHEESE

Toss well-washed torn Boston lettuce leaves with about 18 whole walnut meats broken into bits, and the following vinaigrette. Serve with Cambazola cheese, a mild, creamy blue, topped with a grind of black pepper.

- 1 teaspoon champagne mustard
- 2 tablespoons white wine vinegar
- ½ teaspoon salt
- ¼ teaspoon white pepper
- ¼ cup walnut oil

Whisk all ingredients together.
Makes enough vinaigrette for 6 servings

OPPOSITE: *Mixed lilies.* ABOVE, CLOCKWISE FROM TOP LEFT: *Endive and Radicchio, Mixed Green Salad, Mâche Salad, Chèvre-Stuffed Endive Spears, and Boston Lettuce Salad.*

MACHE SALAD WITH WHITE WINE VINAIGRETTE

Mâche is one of my favorite salad greens. I like it on its own.

12   bunches mâche, roots cut off, washed and dried

2   tablespoons plus 1½ teaspoons white wine vinegar
1   generous teaspoon grainy mustard
½   teaspoon soy sauce
    Black pepper to taste
4   tablespoons olive oil

Tear mâche bunches into several pieces and place in a salad bowl.

Whisk together all other ingredients and dress salad. Top each serving with a grind of black pepper.
Serves 6

149

Five Great Desserts

APPLE-ALMOND CUSTARD

You might substitute some other nut for the almonds and pears for the apples as a variation on this easy dessert.

- 1½   Golden Delicious apples, peeled, cored, and coarsely chopped
- 2   tablespoons sugar
- 2   tablespoons unsalted butter
- 6   tablespoons coarsely ground almonds
- 1   cup milk
- 2   tablespoons honey
- 2   large eggs
- ¼   teaspoon salt
- 1   teaspoon Calvados or vanilla extract

Preheat the oven to 350 degrees. Generously butter six ½-cup ovenproof custard cups. Place cups in an ovenproof pan large enough to hold them comfortably.

Divide the chopped apple among the cups. Sprinkle each with a teaspoon of sugar and place a teaspoon of butter on each. Surround the cups with warm tap water and bake for 25 minutes, until apples are tender and just beginning to brown very slightly. Sprinkle each with a generous tablespoon of ground almonds. Return to oven for another 5 minutes.

Meanwhile, scald the milk and stir in honey. Lightly beat the eggs and pour into the milk, stirring. Add salt and Calvados, mixing well. Strain mixture into the 6 cups, filling each.

Bake for 30 minutes, or until a knife comes out clean when inserted into the middle of the custard. Allow to cool and refrigerate until ready to serve.

To serve, run a knife around the edges of the cups and invert onto individual dessert plates. Holding the cup in place, give it a little shake to get custard to come out.

You may top these with a little sweetened pureed fruit or a dab of spiked whipped cream (or both) if you like. Or you might serve them plain with thin cookies.
Serves 6

—

HAZELNUT JAM CAKE

This is a very sweet cake, so it's best to use a rather tart jelly on it.

- 1   cup peeled hazelnuts
- 1¾   cups all-purpose flour
- ¼   teaspoon baking soda
- ½   cup (1 stick) unsalted butter
- 1½   cups sugar
- 3   large eggs, separated
- ⅔   cup sour cream
- 1   teaspoon vanilla extract
- 8 to 12   ounces tart jelly or jam
- 1   cup heavy cream
- 3   tablespoons of brandy

Preheat the oven to 325 degrees. Grease and lightly flour two 8-inch round cake pans.

In a small skillet, toast the hazelnuts over moderate heat until fragrant, about 3 minutes. Cool, then chop coarsely. In a large bowl, sift the flour with the baking soda. Set aside a few tablespoons of the flour mixture on a plate. In a medium bowl, cream the butter and sugar until light and fluffy, about 3 minutes. Add the egg yolks, one at a time, beating well after each addition.

Add the dry ingredients to the egg and butter mixture alternately with the sour cream, beginning and ending with the flour. Stir in the vanilla and mix.

Lightly dredge the hazelnuts in the reserved flour on the plate, shaking off any excess. Fold into the batter.

In a medium bowl, beat the egg whites until stiff peaks form. Stir one-third of the whites into the batter, then carefully fold in the balance. Pour into prepared pans, shaking to spread thick batter evenly. Bake until golden and a cake tester comes out clean, 40 to 50 minutes. Let layers cool in the pan before turning out.

Brush crumbs off and place one layer on a cake plate. Heat jam so it will be runny. Pour and spread about half over the bottom layer. Top with the second layer and hold in place with toothpicks. Spread the remaining jam over the top and let run over the sides.

Whip the cream to soft peaks and flavor with the brandy. Serve a big dollop with each slice of cake.
Serves 12

—

LIME MOUSSE

Obviously, this may be made with lemon juice.

- 1   envelope unflavored gelatin
- ¼   cup cold water
- ¾   cup fresh lime juice
- ¾   cup sugar
-   Pinch of salt
- 1   generous teaspoon grated lemon rind
- 2   cups heavy cream, whipped to soft peaks

In a ceramic or glass bowl, sprinkle gelatin over the cold water and allow to dissolve. Meanwhile, combine lime juice, sugar, and salt in a small saucepan. Stir in dissolved gelatin and simmer over medium heat for 3 minutes.

Stir in lemon rind and allow to cool and thicken slightly. Fold in whipped cream. Tie an oiled waxed paper collar onto a 4-cup soufflé dish. Pour mixture in and refrigerate until set, several hours.

Serve topped with berries or lemon or vanilla sauce. You might want to serve a tea cookie with it, too. Or just serve it plain.
Serves 6 to 8

Apple-Almond Custard.

MIXED BERRIES WITH VANILLA CREAM

Any combination of berries will do here.

- 1 cup milk
- 3 large egg yolks
- ⅓ cup sugar
- 1½ teaspoons vanilla extract
- 3 cups or more mixed berries

Place the milk in a small saucepan and scald. Beat the yolks and sugar together, then slowly stir into the milk. Pour into a double boiler and cook over hot, not boiling water until thickened slightly and the mixture coats the back of a spoon, about 15 minutes. Stir in the vanilla. Allow to cool, then refrigerate.

Place berries in individual bowls and top with the vanilla cream.

Serves 6

CHOCOLATE MACADAMIA FLAN

This is for Southern chocolate freaks, who seem to like their chocolate desserts milkier than other folks.

- ¾ cup sugar
- 3 tablespoons water
- 1 cup coarsely chopped macadamia nuts, toasted
- 3 large eggs, plus 3 egg yolks
- 3 cups half-and-half
- 6 ounces semisweet chocolate, coarsely chopped
- 1½ teaspoons instant espresso powder
- 1½ teaspoons vanilla extract

Preheat the oven to 300 degrees.

Combine ½ cup sugar with the water in a small saucepan and bring to a boil. Cook over medium-low heat, stirring occasionally, until syrup begins to caramelize, about 6 minutes. When dark golden, pour into a 6-cup metal ring mold. Working quickly and us-ing a pot holder, tilt the mold around to coat the bottom and sides as the syrup cools. When completely cooled, sprinkle with nuts and set aside.

Lightly beat together the eggs and yolks and set aside.

Scald the half-and-half in the top of a double boiler. Stir in the chocolate, remaining sugar, espresso powder, and vanilla. Continue stirring until the chocolate is melted. Slowly pour milk mixture into the eggs, stirring. Pour through a strainer, then into the mold. Place mold in a larger ovenproof pan and surround with boiling water. Bake until set, about 40 to 50 minutes. Allow to cool and refrigerate, covered.

To serve, loosen edges of flan with a knife. Invert onto a serving plate, and if flan doesn't come out with a gentle shake, *very* sharply shake down to unmold.

Serve with a dollop of whipped cream, sweetened slightly and flavored with vanilla, Grand Marnier, or framboise *eau-de-vie.*

Serves 8

ABOVE: *Chocolate Macadamia Flan.* BELOW: *Mixed Berries with Vanilla Cream.*

ABOVE: *Hazelnut Jam Cake.* BELOW: *Lime Mousse.*

ROAST TURKEY WITH PAN GRAVY

CORN BREAD STUFFING

SWEET SQUASH CASSEROLE

TINY GREEN PEAS WITH DILL BUTTER

CRANBERRY, ORANGE, AND RAISIN SAUCE

A Holiday Dinner

Now that I've had my say on how I don't want to stay in the kitchen, let me go on to tell you about when I love being there — Thanksgiving and Christmas. On these holidays I'm a traditionalist through and through. Maybe I've reduced the number of courses, but the menu is always turkey with corn bread stuffing, cranberries, and a couple of vegetables. I've tended to lighten up on desserts in these menus mainly because most guests have already stuffed themselves before they get that far. And besides, think how sanctimonious you feel when you can respond to proffered dessert with "No, no — just a little coffee will be fine." Or "Well, maybe just the smallest sliver. No, no, that's too much."

One pie will usually do for such a bunch (of which I'm a guilty member) — and I usually let someone else bring it.

OPPOSITE AND ABOVE: *Dinner guests.* RIGHT: *Table set for dinner.* BELOW: *Prometheus at Christmastime.*

ROAST TURKEY WITH PAN GRAVY

For openers, order your turkey in advance, and order a fresh one — automatically guaranteeing a better flavor.

Next, remember that the legs and thighs are tougher than the breast meat and take longer to be tenderized by the heat. Also, drumsticks and wings tend to dry out while in the oven if they are not properly secured. So correctly trussing the turkey is important. Simple instructions for doing this may be found in almost any good basic cookbook. My father used to wrap slices of bacon around the lower part of each drumstick — a trick you might try. To keep the breast from drying out, start cooking the turkey with a piece of doubled cheesecloth, about 8 by 12 inches, dipped in melted margarine or butter, stretched over the breast. Leave this protection in place during the roasting period; just remove it for the last hour to allow the breast to brown.

I begin with a very hot oven, 450 degrees, to seal the meat. I reduce the heat to 325 degrees as soon as the turkey goes in. For a fifteen-pound bird, I figure about eighteen minutes a pound, and I baste every thirty minutes with pan juices and additional chicken stock. However, timing can be difficult to gauge because it may vary somewhat according to the age of the bird and heat loss from opening the oven door for basting (and the likelihood that the oven thermostat may be slightly off). For that reason, I use the traditional test of pricking the thighs to see how the juices look after all but about a half-hour of the cooking time has elapsed. Juices must run clear, with no trace of pink, for the meat to be properly done. As an additional test, I use one of those small instant-read thermometers. The reading ought to register around 185 or 190 degrees. Remember a turkey continues to cook after it is removed from the oven.

Once out, leave it to rest for a half-hour, which will make it easier to carve. Don't worry about it getting cold; if the turkey is covered loosely with foil, you will be surprised by how hot it remains. The thirty-minute grace period after roasting will give you ample time to deal with all the other elements of the meal. The sweet squash dish can go in to bake, timed to come out when you want to sit down at the table. This leaves the gravy. Before you start this, skim the fat off carefully. And don't use too much thickener — gravy tends to thicken more while being kept warm. And, finally, be sure to make enough! Last, the peas are quickly heated. The Cranberry, Orange, and Raisin Sauce will have been made the day before.

Now, how to serve the turkey. Of course, you want everyone to see how beautifully cooked it is, but carving the whole thing at the table can be a nightmare without the proper know-how and technique. Even then I think it is still too messy. My solution is a compromise. In the kitchen, I cut off the legs and wings, carving the meat from the thighs while leaving the drumsticks and wings whole. (I do cut the joints of the wings with poultry shears to make them easier to eat.) Next, I remove the stuffing from the body cavity, but leave the stuffed neck untouched. Incidentally, if there is a time lag here, keep the meat and stuffing warm in the oven. When everything is ready to go, I put the turkey, minus its wings and legs, in the center of a warm platter and garnish with whatever strikes my fancy; the dark meat, wings, and drumsticks go around both sides. The breast is easy to carve in the dining room and everyone gets a chance to exclaim over the perfectly cooked bird.

No matter how you do it, by the time the last guests are served, the food will have cooled off a bit, making it doubly important for the gravy to be hot. Ideally, keep the gravy boat over a warming light, and warm the plates if you can swing it. And personally, since a denuded turkey carcass is not the most edifying sight in the world, I think it is best to serve from a sideboard or a small table set up for that purpose, so everything will be more or less out of view while you are dining.

Incidentally, this whole menu calls

The holiday table with Roast Turkey, Tiny Green Peas, the Sweet Squash Casserole, and Cranberry, Orange, and Raisin Sauce.

for lots of butter, but I figure what the heck, this is a once- or twice-a-year meal. However, I have used half butter and half margarine, and I really can't tell the difference. As a matter of fact, I think you could get away with using all margarine in the stuffing.

TURKEY

   1 **15-pound turkey**
      Corn Bread Stuffing
      (page 158)

PAN GRAVY

   3 **tablespoons flour**
   3 **tablespoons unsalted butter,**
      softened
   3 **cups Turkey Stock (page 159)**

Preheat the oven to 450 degrees.

Roast the turkey: Stuff the cavity and neck of the turkey and close the openings securely. Truss. Place the bird on a greased rack in a roasting pan and place in the oven. Turn the heat back to 325 degrees and roast for approximately 4¼ hours (about 18 minutes per pound).

Make the gravy: Press the flour into the butter. Set aside. Heat the stock.

While the turkey is resting after being roasted, deglaze the pan with the heated stock. Skim off whatever fat rises to the top (I use one of those defatting cups, which are pretty handy devices to have). Dissolve just enough of the flour-butter mixture into the liquid to begin to thicken it. Simmer for about 5 minutes.

Taste and correct seasoning if necessary. Pour into a saucepan and reserve. Reheat the gravy before serving.
Serves 10, with leftovers

Note: If you haven't got enough stock left, add some canned chicken stock.

ABOVE: *Rockefeller Center Christmas.* BELOW: *Drinks before dinner.* OPPOSITE: *At table.*

CORN BREAD STUFFING

Yellow Corn Bread (recipe follows)
1½ cups cubed toast (see *Note*)
½ cup (1 stick) unsalted butter
1½ generous cups *each* chopped green bell pepper, onion, and celery
1 large bunch green onions, with some tops, chopped
1 cup coarsely chopped toasted pecans
¼ cup finely chopped fresh parsley
1 tablespoon salt, or to taste
1 teaspoon black pepper
¼ teaspoon cayenne pepper
¼ teaspoon dried thyme
2 to 4 hard-cooked eggs, coarsely shredded
2 large eggs, beaten lightly
1 cup Turkey Stock (recipe follows)

Crumble the corn bread and place it in a large mixing bowl with the toast. Melt half the butter in a large skillet and add the green pepper, onion, celery, and green onions. Cook over very low heat to wilt the vegetables. Meanwhile, toss the pecans, parsley, salt, pepper, cayenne, and thyme with the breads. When the vegetables are wilted, add them to the bread mixture and toss. Carefully mix in the hard-cooked eggs, then the raw eggs. Last, melt the rest of the butter, mix it with the turkey stock, and use this to dampen the stuffing.

Put any stuffing that doesn't fit into the turkey into a well-greased, shallow baking dish. Cover it with foil and bake it with the turkey for the last hour, or bake it separately at 350 degrees for 45 minutes.

Note: I use 5 slices of Pepperidge Farm Toasting White Bread, *well* toasted, to make the cubes.

YELLOW CORN BREAD

I generally make this the night before I want to use it. Then I break it into large chunks and leave it out uncovered so it will get a little stale.

1¼ cups yellow cornmeal
¾ cup all-purpose flour
1 teaspoon sugar
½ teaspoon salt
4 teaspoons baking powder
1 cup milk
1 large egg, lightly beaten
2 tablespoons safflower oil

Preheat the oven to 450 degrees. Place a skillet — cast iron is best — in the oven while it preheats.

When the oven is ready, sift the dry ingredients. Mix the milk, egg, and safflower oil. Add to the sifted ingredients. Mix briefly and lightly; do not overmix.

Remove the skillet from the oven,

coat it with vegetable-oil spray, and add the batter. Return to the oven and reduce the heat to 425 degrees. Bake for 20 to 25 minutes, until golden.

TURKEY STOCK

Since the flavor of both the gravy and the stuffing depends to some degree on the flavor of this stock, make sure it is not bland, but has a rich taste. Add more seasoning and more bouillon cubes or powdered stock if required.

> Turkey neck and giblets
> 1 medium onion, cut in half
> 1 large celery rib, with top, broken into several pieces
> 1 large carrot, broken in half
> Few sprigs of parsley
> 2 bouillon cubes
> 1 quart water
> Salt and black pepper to taste

Put the vegetables in a stock pot. Add water and cook for 1 hour, skimming as necessary. Strain, discarding vegetables and reserving meat. Correct seasoning if necessary and set aside.

Remove meat from the neck, discarding skin, and chop along with giblets. These may be added to the stuffing or the gravy, or divided between the two.

SWEET SQUASH CASSEROLE

I use acorn squash for this, but any sweet winter squash will do.

> 4 medium acorn squash
> 6 to 8 tablespoons (¾ to 1 stick) unsalted butter
> 6 tablespoons Brownulated sugar
> ¼ teaspoon salt
> ½ teaspoon grated nutmeg

Preheat the oven to 350 degrees.

Halve and seed the squash. Rub them lightly with a little of the butter and sprinkle each half with about ½ teaspoon of the Brownulated sugar. Place in a shallow baking pan and bake until tender, about 1 hour.

Allow to cool slightly, then scoop out the flesh. Mash, then beat until

smooth with 4 tablespoons butter, 4 tablespoons sugar, the salt, and the nutmeg. Lightly butter an 8-cup soufflé dish and scrape the squash in. Dot with the remaining butter and sprinkle remaining sugar over it all.

Bake for about 30 minutes, until top is bubbly.

Serves 8 or more

TINY GREEN PEAS WITH DILL BUTTER

I use frozen baby green peas, which I've found don't actually have to be cooked. I place them in a strainer and let them stand in a bowl, covered with boiling water, until they are heated through. This only takes a minute or so. I then shake them dry and continue with the recipe below.

3	12-ounce packages frozen tiny green peas
3	tablespoons minced fresh dill
4 to 6	tablespoons (½ to ¾ stick) unsalted butter, softened
¼	teaspoon sugar
½ to ¾	teaspoon salt, or to taste

Prepare the peas as indicated above. Meanwhile, mash dill into the softened butter. Combine hot peas with the dill butter, sugar, and salt.
Serves 8 or more

———

CRANBERRY, ORANGE, AND RAISIN SAUCE

This is a slight variation on the old favorite relish.

4	cups fresh cranberries, about 1 pound
1	large seedless orange
2	cups sugar
1½	cups golden raisins
¾	cup fresh orange juice

The day before, wash and pick over cranberries. Cut the orange into eighths. Place in a food processor with the cranberries and chop coarsely. Stir in the sugar and refrigerate overnight. Place the raisins in a small bowl and cover with orange juice. Macerate overnight. Combine cranberry-orange mixture with macerated raisins and orange juice. Stir to mix.
Serves 8 or more

OPPOSITE: *Central Park.* TOP: *The Pulitzer Fountain.* RIGHT: *The Sherry-Netherland clock.*

Sunday Lunch

O NCE IN A BLUE MOON I'll have friends in to lunch on Sunday. So here's something I like that makes a delightful lunch if it's the right season. As for drinks, adding a few drops of any *eau-de-vie* to a glass of champagne makes a festive prelunch cocktail.

CHAMPAGNE WITH EAU-DE-VIE

BROCCOLI RABE SOUP

WARM SOFT-SHELL CRAB SALAD

PECAN CRUST
BUTTERSCOTCH PIE

BROCCOLI RABE SOUP

Frankly, you have to know your guests' tastes to serve this soup. Broccoli rabe, which I love, can be very bitter — too bitter for some — so if you and your guests don't much like its flavor, substitute spinach.

1 large bunch fresh broccoli rabe, stems trimmed
3 cups chicken stock
2 tablespoons unsalted butter
1 medium onion, coarsely diced
1 large potato, peeled and diced
Salt and black pepper to taste
Lemon slices (optional)
Sour cream or crème fraîche (optional)

Wash the broccoli rabe and place in a covered saucepan with just the water clinging to it. Add about ½ cup of the chicken stock and cook slowly until tender, about 20 minutes.

Meanwhile, melt the butter in a skillet and sauté the onion until tender, about 5 minutes. Add the potato and the balance of the chicken stock. Cover and simmer until potato is tender, about 12 minutes. Strain out potato and onion, saving liquid, and combine with the cooked broccoli rabe and its liquid. Puree. Return to saucepan and add reserved liquid. Heat and correct seasoning with salt and pepper. You may add more stock if soup is too thick.

Serve in warm bowls garnished with a slice of lemon and/or a dollop of sour cream or crème fraîche.
Serves 6

WARM SOFT-SHELL CRAB SALAD

Soft-shell crabs cook quickly, so have everything ready (the vinaigrette made so it only has to reheat) and get back in the kitchen right after the soup. You can have the salad on the table in ten minutes.

- 6 cleaned soft-shell crabs
  Milk
- 2 strips thick bacon, cut into ¼-inch pieces
- 4 tablespoons olive oil
- 1 tablespoon balsamic vinegar
- 1½ tablespoons red wine vinegar
  Salt and black pepper to taste
- ¼ teaspoon Worcestershire sauce
- 1 teaspoon fresh lemon juice
- 8 cups mixed salad greens, well washed
- ⅓ cup all-purpose flour
- ⅓ cup cornmeal
- 4 tablespoons (½ stick) unsalted butter
- 6 large green onions, chopped, with some green
  Lemon wedges for garnish

Place crabs in a small bowl and cover with milk. Set aside, but don't refrigerate after combining. (This may be done an hour in advance.)

Fry the bacon pieces until crisp. Drain. Reserve 1 tablespoon of the bacon fat and discard the balance. Wipe out skillet and add the fat, 3 tablespoons of olive oil, the vinegars, salt, pepper, and Worcestershire sauce. Whisk together and set this vinaigrette aside.

Combine the remaining tablespoon of olive oil and the lemon juice. Toss with the salad greens. Salt and pepper lightly. Arrange on large individual salad plates, then set aside.

Combine the flour, cornmeal, salt, and pepper on a sheet of waxed paper. Drain the crabs and pat dry (discard milk). Dredge each in the flour-corn-meal mixture. Shake off excess. Melt butter over medium heat in a skillet large enough to hold all the crabs. Meanwhile, put the vinaigrette over very low heat to warm it. When the butter is hot, just past the bubbly stage, add the crabs, underside down. Sauté for 2½ minutes, turn, and sauté another 2½ minutes, adjusting the heat if necessary and shaking the pan. Large crabs may require another minute or so, but do not overcook.

Place a crab on the center of each bed of greens, then sprinkle with the bacon and green onions. Spoon a tablespoon of the hot vinaigrette over each crab. Garnish with lemon wedges and serve immediately.
Serves 6

OPPOSITE: *In the studio.* BELOW: *Broccoli Rabe Soup.*

PECAN CRUST BUTTERSCOTCH PIE

I think nut crusts are too often over-looked. They're easy to make and you may use any kind of nut, or a combination of several. And nut crusts are marvelous with almost any cream pie. Experiment!

Note that you use toasted nuts in the filling as well as the crust, so do the whole batch at once. Also, when you use an egg white in the crust, save the yolk to go into the filling.

PASTRY
- 1½ generous cups finely chopped toasted nuts (see *Note*)
- ¼ cup sugar
- White of 1 large egg

FILLING
- 1 cup light brown sugar, tightly packed
- ½ cup all-purpose flour
- ¼ teaspoon salt
- 2 cups milk
- 3 large egg yolks
- 3 tablespoons unsalted butter
- 1½ teaspoons vanilla extract
- ½ cup coarsely chopped toasted pecans
- 1 cup heavy cream
- 1 tablespoon rum

Preheat the oven to 350 degrees. Lightly coat a 9-inch pie pan with vegetable-oil spray.

Make the pastry: Combine the nuts and sugar, then stir in the egg white, mixing well. Mound in the center of the pie pan. Pat gently to cover bottom and sides evenly. Rinse hands in cold water if they become sticky, leaving them damp, and continue patting crust in place.

Bake until set, about 20 minutes. Place on a rack until completely cool. When you first remove crust from the oven, if it has puffed up in spots, gently pat it back down while it is still hot.

Make the filling: Place the brown sugar, flour, and salt in a bowl and combine well. In another bowl, whisk together ½ cup milk and the egg yolks. Whisk this into the sugar-flour mixture, then add the balance of the milk and combine well.

Place in the top of a double boiler and cook over barely boiling water, whisking, until very thick, 12 to 15 minutes. Off the heat, stir in butter and vanilla, then the pecans.

Cover with a round of waxed paper, placed directly on the surface. Let filling cool about 15 minutes, then pour it into the crust. Cover as before with waxed paper; when it reaches room temperature, chill it for at least 3 hours.

Whip the cream lightly and stir in the rum. Place a big spoonful on top of each piece before serving.
Serves 8

Note: To toast nuts, place in a low-sided baking pan. Bake in a 350 degree oven for about 8 to 10 minutes, until starting to turn color, stirring if necessary to keep from burning. Allow to cool before using.

ABOVE: *Pecan Crust Butterscotch Pie.* RIGHT: *Warm Soft-Shell Crab Salad.*

In St Barth's

I'VE BEEN RENTING HOUSES in the Caribbean off and on for almost two decades now, so I suppose — in some ways at least — I'm an old hand. One of the things I've come to realize, and value, from these years of experience is the comfort of familiar surroundings. While there's certainly fun in the adventure of discovering the quirks and crannies of a new place, there are sure to be problems as well as delights. So on your first extended visit to a house be prepared for the drawbacks that always accompany the unexpected pleasures. Obviously by returning several times, you have the security of having learned how to cope with the inconveniences.

But why complain? There's all that warm blue water and sunshine, those beaches and flowers, and unhurried days ending with those almost ridiculously perfect sunsets. So what if the kitchen is prehistoric? Improvising is part of the game. And an island such as St. Barth's offers lots to improvise with. Because it's French, there are good staples to work with — breads, sweet butter, cheeses, ham, crème fraîche, pâtés, sausages, lots of "good enough" wine, and even an array of fresh vegetables and other produce when you learn when various stores get their shipments.

So here are some recipes to inspire you and some typical menus, which have evolved over many visits.

LEFT: *Island meadow.* ABOVE: *In the library.*

Pasta Variations

THANK HEAVEN for pasta. It pleases everyone and may be sauced with almost anything. When we first arrive, we usually make a big batch of simple tomato sauce that we then utilize in various ways. So to put together a quick and easy meal, pick a sauce recipe — all you need add is a loaf of crusty bread, a good salad, and cheese (if you are not sprinkling Parmesan on top of the pasta), a bottle of wine, and store-bought ice cream and cookies. These portions are heartier than those in the chapter on Tuscany. Maybe it's the sea air.

BELOW: *Farfalle with Grilled Chicken Breasts and Cubed Chèvre.* OPPOSITE TOP: *Spaghetti with Tuna, Olives, Capers, and Cayenne.* OPPOSITE BOTTOM: *Penne with Mixed Grilled Vegetables.*

BASIC TOMATO SAUCE

This recipe may easily be halved or cut into thirds.

- ¼ cup olive oil
- 3 cups chopped onions
- 1¾ to 2 cups shredded carrots
- 1 heaping tablespoon minced garlic
- 12 cups canned peeled tomatoes (no paste) with their juice
- 2½ teaspoons salt, or to taste
- 1 teaspoon black pepper
- 1 teaspoon dried basil

Heat the oil in a deep pot. Sauté the onions and carrots over medium-high heat until wilted, 4 to 5 minutes. Stir in garlic. Add tomatoes and bring to a simmer. Stir in salt, pepper, and basil. Simmer to reduce and thicken, about 15 minutes. Do not overcook.
Makes 12 plus cups

SPAGHETTI WITH TUNA, OLIVES, CAPERS, AND CAYENNE

- 3 cups Basic Tomato Sauce, heated
- 1 cup sliced stuffed green olives
- 6 tablespoons capers, drained
- 1 6½-ounce can tuna, in oil, drained
  Cayenne pepper to taste
- 1½ pounds spaghetti
- 2 tablespoons unsalted butter
  Freshly grated Parmesan cheese

Heat the tomato sauce and stir in the olives, capers, and tuna, breaking tuna chunks with a fork. Add cayenne and set aside.

Cook the spaghetti in plenty of well-salted water. When it's cooked *al dente*, drain it. Add the butter to the pot and dump hot, drained pasta in, tossing. Add 1½ cups of sauce to the balance to the pasta and toss. Top each serving with ¼ cup of the remaining sauce and a sprinkling of Parmesan.
Serves 6

FARFALLE WITH GRILLED CHICKEN BREASTS AND CUBED CHEVRE

- 3 large boned chicken breasts, cut in half
- 6 tablespoons fresh lime juice
- 6 tablespoons olive oil
- 3 large garlic cloves, sliced thin
- 1½ pounds farfalle (bowtie) pasta
- 2 tablespoons unsalted butter
- 2 cups Basic Tomato Sauce, heated
- 1½ cups cubed chèvre (goat) cheese
  Black pepper

Place the chicken in a shallow dish. Whisk together the lime juice, oil, and garlic; pour over chicken. Cover and marinate for at least 2 hours, in the refrigerator, turning once. Grill until done over coals or under the broiler, about 5 to 7 minutes per side. (It depends on how hot the coals are and how close the chicken is to them.) Do not overcook.

Meanwhile, put pasta on to cook in plenty of well-salted water. When it's *al dente* drain it and add butter to pot. Dump pasta back in and toss. Add sauce and toss, then add cheese and toss again. Place on individual warm plates. Skin the chicken breast halves, discarding skin, and slice. Place on top of each plate of pasta. Top with a grind or two of black pepper.

Serves 6

PENNE WITH MIXED GRILLED VEGETABLES

- **6 thick slices of peeled eggplant
  Salt**
- **3 medium leeks, well washed, blanched 5 minutes**
- **6 large diagonal slices of zucchini**
- **3 medium red bell peppers, cut into quarters, lengthwise, and seeded
  Olive oil
  Salt and black pepper to taste**
- **1½ pounds penne**

- **2 tablespoons unsalted butter**
- **2 cups Basic Tomato Sauce, heated
  Balsamic vinegar, to taste**

Sprinkle the eggplant slices generously with salt and allow to drain for 30 minutes. Wash off salt and pat dry.

Cut blanched leeks in half lengthwise. Rub the vegetables generously with olive oil. Place zucchini and peppers on the grill. Sprinkle with salt and pepper. Cook about 1 minute, then add eggplant slices and leeks. Sprinkle with salt and pepper. Cook all about 4 minutes longer, turning and sprinkling other sides with salt and pepper.

Meanwhile, cook pasta in plenty of well-salted water. When it's *al dente*, drain it and add butter to pot. Dump pasta back in and toss. Add tomato sauce and toss.

Cut vegetables into large chunks. Put pasta on individual plates and top each

with vegetables. Sprinkle vegetables with a little balsamic or red wine vinegar.

Serves 6

LEFTOVERS

A good way to utilize leftover pasta is to toss it with a little of the sauce, then put it into a well-buttered, shallow baking dish. (The dish may be refrigerated at this point.) To finish, beat 5 or 6 eggs with some of the sauce and extra salt and pepper. Pour this over the pasta and top with grated Emmental cheese and soft bread crumbs. Dot with butter. Bake at 350 degrees until set, about 15 minutes or so. Run under the broiler to turn golden. Serve with extra tomato sauce on the side, salad, and store-bought dessert.

OPPOSITE: *Looking down on the beach.* ABOVE: *Island flowers.*

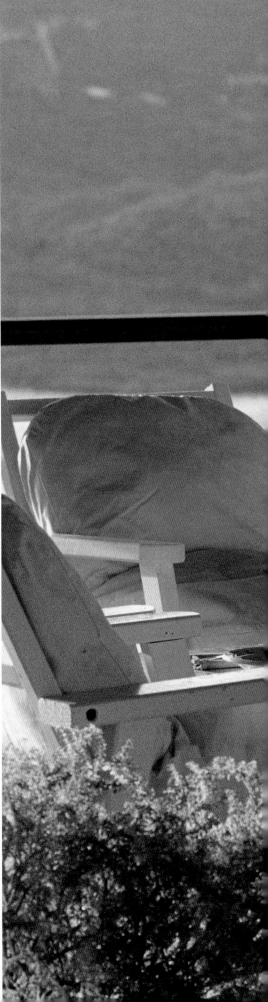

An Egg Dish

HERE IS ANOTHER fast and uncomplicated menu — centered on an egg dish, which is my version of a frittata. Like the pasta meals, all you require is a salad and dessert, which in this case is a lime meringue pie.

SKILLET POTATOES AND EGGS WITH SWEET
CHILI PEPPERS AND HAM

SLICED AVOCADO SALAD WITH MUSTARD VINAIGRETTE

TOASTED FRENCH BREAD SLICES

LIME MERINGUE PIE

TOP: *Skillet Potatoes and Eggs with Sweet Chili Peppers and Ham.*
ABOVE: *Avocado Salad.* RIGHT: *On the covered terrace.*

SKILLET POTATOES AND EGGS WITH SWEET CHILI PEPPERS AND HAM

Actually, I cheated a little here. Canned sweet green chili peppers aren't available on the island that I know of, but since I like them I usually throw a couple of cans in my suitcase. You may want to sprinkle grated cheese on top just as it goes under the broiler.

- **2 medium potatoes, peeled**
- **2 tablespoons vegetable oil**
- **½ teaspoon salt, or to taste**
  Black pepper to taste
- **8 large eggs, lightly beaten**
- **2 tablespoons clarified unsalted butter**
- **1 generous cup medium to small cubes of cooked ham**
- **¾ cup chopped drained mild green chilies (canned)**

Boil the potatoes in well-salted water. When medium-tender, drain them and allow to cool. Dice into medium to small chunks. Heat oil over medium heat in a medium skillet. Sauté potatoes until they begin to brown, about 5 minutes. Remove to a plate and wipe out skillet.

Preheat the broiler. Salt and pepper the eggs. Mix well. Add clarified butter to skillet and heat over medium heat. When bubbly, add eggs. Stir lightly as they begin to set. Sprinkle in the potatoes, ham, and chilies while the eggs are still liquid. Mix very lightly.

Run under the broiler for a minute or so until puffed and golden.
Serves 4 to 6

———

SLICED AVOCADO SALAD WITH MUSTARD VINAIGRETTE

You may vary this vinaigrette by using salt instead of the soy sauce and mashing in a couple of anchovy filets.

LEFT: *Lime Meringue Pie.* ABOVE: *End of the day.*

3 ripe avocados, peeled, pitted, and sliced
¼ teaspoon black pepper
1 teaspoon soy sauce, or to taste
2 tablespoons fresh lemon juice
1 generous teaspoon grainy mustard
5 tablespoons olive oil
½ small red onion, cut into thin rings

Slice the avocados thickly and rub each slice with a little extra lemon juice to prevent from turning dark. Place in a salad bowl.

Meanwhile, place pepper, soy sauce, lemon juice, and mustard in a small bowl and whisk together. Whisk in oil.

Spoon sauce over avocados or serve on the side. Garnish with red onion rings. *Serves 6*

LIME MERINGUE PIE

Since the limes are so good and plentiful here, we make a custard pie from them. This recipe makes enough for two crusts. Freeze half the dough for later.

PASTRY
2½ cups all-purpose flour
3 tablespoons sugar
   Pinch of salt
12 tablespoons (1½ sticks) unsalted butter, cut into pieces and chilled
4 tablespoons vegetable shortening, chilled
6 tablespoons ice water

FILLING
1½ cups superfine sugar
¼ cup plus 1 tablespoon cornstarch
¼ teaspoon salt
4 large eggs, separated, plus 1 egg white
½ cup fresh lime juice
2 cups cold water
1½ teaspoons grated lemon zest
5 tablespoons unsalted butter, cut into 5 pieces

Make the pastry: Mix all the dry ingredients. Add the butter and vegetable shortening, cutting in with 2 knives or a pastry blender until mixture resembles coarse meal. Sprinkle water over all and mix with a fork until dough clings to-gether. Form into 2 balls and flatten each between 2 sheets of waxed paper. Chill the one you are going to use for at least 30 minutes before rolling it out; freeze the other half.

Preheat the oven to 400 degrees.

Roll out the dough and line an 8-inch pie pan. Crimp the edges. Line pan with foil and fill bottom of pan with pie weights, raw rice, or dry beans. Place in oven and cook until crust is set, about 10 minutes. Remove foil and weights. Reduce heat to 350 degrees and continue to bake until crust is golden, 10 to 15 minutes. Puncture any bubbles that appear in the dough as it bakes. Allow to cool before filling.

Make the filling: In a large, heavy saucepan combine 1 cup of the sugar, the cornstarch, salt, 4 egg yolks, and lime juice. Add the water and whisk until blended. Cook over moderate heat, whisking constantly, until mixture comes to a boil. Boil, whisking, for 1 minute, then remove from heat. Add zest and butter, stirring until melted. Either press a sheet of plastic wrap on the finished filling or rub it with a little extra butter to keep a hard skin from forming on the top. Set aside.

Preheat the oven to 350 degrees.

Beat the 5 egg whites until foamy. Sprinkle the remaining sugar and a pinch of salt over all. Beat until stiff peaks form. Pour filling into crust and smooth. Top with meringue, sealing it to the pie crust all around.

Bake until golden, about 5 minutes. Allow to cool before serving.
Serves 6 to 8

A "Whole-Meal" Salad

WHAT WOULD WE DO without catch-all salads? Luckily these "whole-meal" dishes seem to suit almost everybody, and with garnishes they can be as simple or as complicated as you choose.

WHITE BEAN AND PASTA SALAD
WITH GARNISHES

ONION AND BLACK OLIVE PIZZA
BREAD

MIXED FRUIT

WHITE BEAN AND PASTA SALAD WITH GARNISHES

I like white bean salads bound together with a slightly mayonnaisey dressing that has just a bit of catsup in it. However, a simple mustard vinaigrette can be just fine.

I like to eat this sort of salad before it has to be refrigerated, so I have the ingredients together at more or less room temperature before I make and add the dressing. Refrigerating just seems to blunt the flavors.

2	cups cooked white beans, drained (see *Note*)
2	cups cooked small elbow macaroni
1	cup drained small green peas
½ to ¾	cup medium-chopped red onion
¼	cup thinly sliced dill pickle or cornichon
1	4-ounce jar chopped pimientos, drained
1½	cups coarsely chopped cooked pork sausage
1	teaspoon salt
½	teaspoon black pepper
1	teaspoon sugar
3	tablespoons red wine vinegar
6	tablespoons olive oil
¼	cup prepared mayonnaise
2	teaspoons catsup

Toss together the beans, pasta, peas, red onion, pickle, pimientos, and sausage.

In a small bowl, combine the salt, pepper, sugar, and vinegar. Mix well with a fork. Whip in olive oil, mayonnaise, and catsup. Pour over salad and toss to coat all ingredients. Serve with garnishes.

Garnishes: All the markets in St. Barth's have lots of tinned goods on their shelves, so we use that French staple, canned petits pois, in the salad. Then as one of the garnishes, we use canned beets tossed with shredded carrots and a little oil and vinegar. Other possible garnishes are hard-cooked eggs, sliced cucumbers, avocado, and sweet bell peppers.
Serves 8, generously

Note: Soak a package of dried white beans overnight. Drain, wash, and cover with about 2 inches of chicken stock (we use boullion cubes). Add a bay leaf or two and simmer, skimming, until tender, up to 1½ hours. Allow to cool in the liquid. When cool, cover and refrigerate.

OPPOSITE: *The "Whole-Meal" Salad.* BELOW: *Onion and Black Olive Pizza Bread.* OVERLEAF: *The far side of the island.*

ONION AND BLACK OLIVE PIZZA BREAD

You can use any topping on this you fancy — just like a regular pizza. This makes enough dough for 2 loaves, so freeze half.

DOUGH
1   package active dry yeast
    Pinch of sugar
1   cup warm water
3   cups all-purpose flour
1   teaspoon salt
¼   cup olive oil

TOPPING
1   small onion, halved and sliced
2   tablespoons olive oil
12 to 18   black oil-cured olives, pitted and coarsely chopped, tossed in a bowl with about 1 tablespoon of their own oil
    Salt and pepper to taste

Make the dough: In a small bowl, combine yeast, sugar, and water. Allow to sit for about 15 minutes, until foamy.

Combine flour and salt in a large bowl. Stir olive oil into the yeast mixture, then add to the flour, mixing well. Add a bit more flour if the dough is too damp. Turn dough out onto a floured surface and knead it lightly for a few minutes. Dough should be soft and elastic.

Oil a large bowl and place dough in it, oil the top of the dough, cover it, and allow it to rise in a warm, draft-free spot until doubled in size, about 45 minutes.

Make the topping: When ready to assemble bread, preheat the oven to 400 degrees and divide dough into 2 balls. Wrap one tightly in plastic wrap and refrigerate (for up to 2 days) or freeze. Oil a small pizza pan, about 12 inches, and roll out the dough to fit it. Pat the dough in place, leaving a thick border all around. Brush dough with 1 tablespoon of the olive oil. Toss onion with the remaining oil. Sprinkle oiled onion over dough and then sprinkle on the olives. Salt and pepper to taste and bake until golden, about 20 minutes.
Makes 1 pizza bread

A Soup Meal

YOU CAN SOMETIMES buy smoked salmon on the island; when it turns up we'll often have smoked salmon chowder for a Sunday treat at lunch, followed by salad made of that Gallic favorite, canned white asparagus. Then for dessert, grilled pineapple with rum cream sauce. All easy but all a little bit special.

SMOKED SALMON AND CORN CHOWDER

ROLLS AND SWEET BUTTER

WHITE ASPARAGUS SALAD WITH PIMIENTO VINAIGRETTE

GRILLED PINEAPPLE WITH RUM CREAM SAUCE

OPPOSITE: *Table set for a soup meal.* LEFT: *Oleander.* BELOW: *Palms in the breeze.*

SMOKED SALMON AND CORN CHOWDER

Obviously this may be made without corn, but I like corn with salmon. You could add small oysters, too.

> 3 tablespoons unsalted butter
> ½ to ⅔ cup finely chopped onion
> ½ to ⅔ cup finely chopped celery
> ½ to ⅔ cup finely chopped red bell pepper
> 2 tablespoons flour
> 3 cups hot chicken stock
> 2 cups low-fat milk
> ½ teaspoon salt
> Black pepper to taste
> 2 cups canned or frozen whole kernel corn, drained

> 4 ounces smoked salmon, chopped into pea-size pieces
> Chopped fresh parsley, dill, or chervil to taste

Melt the butter in a large saucepan. Sauté the onion, celery, and red bell pepper over medium heat until wilted and onion is just beginning to brown, about 8 to 10 minutes. Stir in flour and cook, stirring constantly, for another minute or so. Add the chicken stock and cook for 2 to 3 minutes, stirring. Add the milk and turn heat back to a simmer. Cook for 3 to 4 minutes, stirring occasionally. Add salt, pepper, and corn. Bring back to a simmer and turn off heat. Stir in salmon. Serve with a sprinkling of chopped herbs.

If you prefer a thinner soup, use more chicken stock or milk.
Serves 6

WHITE ASPARAGUS SALAD WITH PIMIENTO VINAIGRETTE

One large can of long white asparagus will usually be enough for 6 servings.

> 1 large can white asparagus
> ½ teaspoon salt, or to taste
> ¼ teaspoon black pepper
> 1 teaspoon Dijon-style mustard
> 2 tablespoons white wine vinegar

5 tablespoons olive oil
5 generous tablespoons pureed pimiento, plus minced pimiento for garnish (optional)
18 black oil-cured olives
Black pepper to taste

Arrange the asparagus on plates.

Place the salt, pepper, mustard, and vinegar in a bowl and whisk. Whisk in the oil, then the pimiento.

Spread a few spoonfuls of the vinaigrette on each serving and a little minced pimiento. Garnish with black olives and top all with black pepper.

Serves 6

GRILLED PINEAPPLE WITH RUM CREAM SAUCE

This delicious rum sauce can be used on baked or grilled bananas.

1 large ripe pineapple, peeled, cored, and cut into 12 lengthwise strips
Clarified unsalted butter
4 tablespoons (½ stick) unsalted butter
½ cup dark brown sugar
½ cup heavy cream
¼ cup light rum
¼ cup fresh lime juice

Dip the pineapple spears in clarified butter and grill 5 minutes on both sides.

LEFT: *Smoked Salmon and Corn Chowder.* TOP: *White Asparagus Salad.* ABOVE: *Grilled Pineapple.*

Meanwhile, combine the 4 tablespoons butter, brown sugar, and cream in a small saucepan. Bring to a boil over medium heat. When all the sugar is melted (almost at the same time it comes to a boil), remove from heat and stir in rum and lime juice. Place 2 slices of pineapple on each serving plate and spoon sauce over. Garnish with thin slices of lime if desired.

Serves 6

A Special Breakfast

EVEN PEOPLE who ordinarily don't eat much breakfast will be delighted to have a special one when they are on a holiday. So here is mine, using the island's ubiquitous crème fraîche to make pancakes.

FRESH ORANGE JUICE

CREME FRAICHE PANCAKES

SAUTEED APPLES

HAZELNUT HONEY BUTTER

BACON

ASSORTED SYRUPS AND JAMS

CREME FRAÎCHE PANCAKES

This recipe makes a very thin and very light pancake.

- 4 large eggs
- ½ teaspoon salt
- 1 teaspoon baking soda
- ½ cup all-purpose flour
- 2 tablespoons sugar
- 2 cups crème fraîche
- 2 tablespoons unsalted butter, melted
- Vegetable oil to grease griddle

Place all the ingredients except the butter and oil into a blender. Blend until smooth, pouring in butter. This takes only 15 or 20 seconds. Stir once to make sure it is all mixed.

Grease a well-heated griddle with vegetable oil. Pour out a scant ¼ cup of batter. When the bubbles on top burst, turn the pancake. Continue, greasing the griddle as necessary.

Serve with Sautéed Apples, Hazelnut Honey Butter, and syrups and jams.
Makes about 18 4-inch pancakes

SAUTÉED APPLES

Sautéed apples are also good served with sausages and cornbread for an easy cold-weather meal.

- 1 tablespoon unsalted butter
- 1 tablespoon vegetable oil
- 3 firm apples, cored, peeled, and cut into 6 lengthwise slices
- 3 tablespoons Brownulated sugar

Heat the butter and oil in a large skillet over high heat and add the apple slices, tossing to coat. Brown lightly, turning, until tender, about 5 minutes. Pour off any liquid or fat and sprinkle brown sugar over all. Stir and toss lightly until well coated.
Serves 6

HAZELNUT HONEY BUTTER

Naturally, you may make this with other kinds of nuts.

- ½ cup (1 stick) unsalted butter, softened
- ½ cup finely chopped toasted hazelnuts
- ¼ cup honey

Combine all the ingredients in a small bowl. Mix well. Refrigerate if not using immediately.
Makes 1 generous cup

OPPOSITE TOP: *Sunday morning breakfast.* OPPOSITE BOTTOM: *Crème Fraîche Pancakes with Sautéed Apples and Bacon.* BELOW: *Fresh orange juice.*

LEFT: *Across the bay.* ABOVE: *Allamonda.* BELOW: *Island cactus.*

AT HOME BY MYSELF

I'M NOT SURE THE MEALS I fix when I'm alone at home can truly be called menus. My weird eating habits started early, when I was about seven years old, I think. Here is how it went, as far as I can remember.

After my maternal grandfather died, my grandmother, "Mawmaw," moved from Argyle Plantation, where I was born, into "town," a community of about 2,000. This was Melville, on the Atchafalaya River in south-central Louisiana. In those days the little town was on the principal route to New Orleans, some 200 miles to the south. There

at Melville automobiles had to cross the river by ferry before going on down to the Crescent City. There was a train bridge though, and the tracks that lead up to it had been laid along the top of the levee that surrounded the village. This levee was necessary to protect the town from the floods that periodically swept the region.

Number 24, the train to New Orleans, passed through Bunkie, which was thirty miles up the line from Melville and where I lived with my parents. By the time I was seven, I was allowed to take it down to Mawmaw's house by myself. Between

Bunkie and Melville there were four stops — not exactly a bullet train but there was lots of bustle (it seemed to me) and things to see. The same conductor and porters who were always on board made sure I was okay and got off where I was supposed to. They all recognized Parson, who never failed to meet me at the Melville depot with Miss Woo, a great white dog, at his side. Parson was about as old as a person can be and still look like a person. He had only one arm and, as unreal as it is to remember now, he had been born into slavery. He had worked for almost sixty years for my grandfather and, before that, my grandfather's family. He came into town with my grandmother when she moved and she gave him a little house in the far corner of her sprawling garden in which to live out his days.

Anyway, the two of us would walk back to the house with Miss Woo running ahead and circling around us. The only one she really loved and had any respect for was Parson, who was so skinny she could have knocked him over in a minute. But when he called out to Miss Woo, or scolded her in his hoarse crackle, she would mind him, returning beseechingly with her head down to receive his forgiveness for her sins of boisterousness.

My grandmother, on the other hand, was too stern for Miss Woo's tastes, and being a woman contented with her settled state, had very little patience with M. W.'s girlish enthusiasm and foolishness. I once heard Mawmaw remark, "That grown dog is so silly, she thinks she's still a puppy."

OPPOSITE: *Me at the refrigerator.* ABOVE: *Iced tea.*

Through the dew-covered bitterweeds we'd go, as I would chatter on about my train ride adventures, to where my grandmother waited. She lived alone and had long ago sensibly realized I was the most marvelous grandchild a person could ever wish for. After lots of kissing and hugging and having my still almost white hair smoothed (I was known as — what else? — "Cotton Top"), I'd be told to go out into the garden to pick the reddest, ripest, best tomato I could find.

By the time I got back, lunch would be ready. You see, my grandmother knew that — although it was just barely ten in the morning — after such an arduous journey her darling would be exhausted and famished.

Lunch consisted of my favorite things: tomatoes with homemade mayonnaise (one of my most prized finds), popcorn, iced tea, and watermelon for dessert. This, Mawmaw unflinchingly ate as though she too had just arrived along with me, starved after the same hair-raising trip, and famished for *her* favorite meal.

Parson was never too crazy about this meal, but he would take a handful or two of popcorn back to his house to enjoy at a much more civilized hour.

So, is it any wonder—?

I know some people cook a proper meal for themselves when they eat alone. Not me.

The following is a sample of what I have either for lunch or dinner when I'm at home by myself working or just goofing off. As for leftovers, I usually eat them until they're gone — or freeze them.

191

ICED TEA

I don't imagine anyone really needs to be told how to make iced tea — except when I make it, I sweeten the whole batch and give it a squeeze of lemon, so that my second glass will taste as good as the first.

———

MUSTARD GREENS

TOASTED CORN BREAD

GREEN ONIONS

SLICED FRESH TOMATOES

MUSTARD GREENS

I prepare broccoli rabe the same way as I do these greens. Mustard greens is one of those rare vegetables that freezing doesn't destroy. Same for broccoli rabe. So when I cook a batch, I freeze individual servings for a quick lunch or dinner.

- 1 bunch mustard greens, washed, with large stems removed
- 1 packet chicken stock powder
- ½ cup hot water
  Black pepper to taste

Leave the water clinging to the washed greens and place greens in a large pot. Dissolve stock in hot water and pour over all. Cover and cook over medium heat, lifting and turning the greens several times as they wilt and cook. They will reduce considerably. Cook until tender, which will depend on how young the greens are — anywhere from 10 to 25 minutes. Add pepper to taste. *Serves 5 to 6*

TOASTED CORN BREAD

This is the basic corn bread recipe I use all the time. I make a batch, cut it into serving pieces, and split them. I then put the split pieces back together and freeze each serving individually wrapped. I split them in advance because I can separate the two sides while they are still frozen and toast them in the toaster right away. If you don't split each serving in advance, you have to thaw it before you can split and toast it. And who wants to wait when he needs corn bread?

Also, I make this in two skillets because I like the corn bread thin so that it will be crisp when I toast it. You can do it in one large skillet if you like. Of course, in that case the split halves will have to be toasted under the broiler.

- 2 cups white cornmeal
- 4 teaspoons baking powder
- 1½ teaspoons salt
- 1½ cups milk (see *Note*)
- 1 large egg, lightly beaten
- 2 tablespoons vegetable oil

Preheat the oven to 425 degrees and place two 9-inch iron skillets in the oven as it preheats. It's important for the skillets to be very hot, so I usually put them in the oven 30 minutes before I use them.

Meanwhile, sift together the cornmeal, baking powder, and salt. Mix the milk, egg, and oil. When the skillets are heated, combine the dry and wet ingredients, stirring. Do not overmix.

Working quickly, coat the inside of each heated skillet with vegetable-oil spray and divide the batter between the pans, smooth the top, and bake until golden, 20 to 25 minutes. *Serves 6 to 8*

Note: You may use sour milk, or a combination of milk and sour cream, instead of fresh milk. When you do, substitute ¼ teaspoon baking soda for ¼ teaspoon baking powder and follow the directions. When substituting sour cream, the batter might be a bit thick, so it should be thinned with an addition of ¼ cup milk or more.

SLICED FRESH TOMATOES

Let me repeat it: If I don't have vine-ripened tomatoes, I don't eat tomatoes.

WARM CHICKEN SALAD WITH HAZELNUT VINAIGRETTE

MELBA TOAST

WARM CHICKEN SALAD WITH HAZELNUT VINAIGRETTE

Once in a while I find myself working at home with someone. When I do, this is something I often have for the two of us to eat. It can be easily varied.

- 1 small chicken breast, skinned and cut in half lengthwise
- 1 small garlic clove, crushed
- 5 tablespoons plus 1 teaspoon hazelnut oil
  Salt and pepper to taste
- 2 tablespoons white wine vinegar
- ¾ teaspoon Dijon-style mustard
- 1 heaping teaspoon minced shallots
- 2 or more cups shredded salad greens

Flatten the chicken halves slightly between 2 sheets of waxed paper, rub them with garlic, and then with 4 teaspoons of the hazelnut oil. Sprinkle with salt and pepper, cover, and refrigerate for at least 1 hour. Preheat the broiler or prepare coals for grilling.

Cook chicken in broiler or on grill very close to the heat for 3 to 4 minutes per side, or until done but not dry. Do not overcook.

Meanwhile, whisk together the balance of the oil, the vinegar, mustard, and add salt and pepper to taste. Stir in the shallots.

Toss the greens with just enough vinaigrette to coat them well. Arrange on 2 large plates. Place grilled chicken on the greens directly from the grill and spoon a little extra vinaigrette over the top of each breast.

You may also sprinkle the chicken with crumbled bacon, toasted chopped hazelnuts, or cheese — or all three. *Serves 2*

Mustard Greens; Warm Chicken Salad with Hazelnut Vinaigrette; Tiny Fresh Asparagus; and Hot Chicken Sandwich.

HOT CHICKEN SANDWICH

SLICED FRESH TOMATOES

STUFFED GREEN OLIVES

SWEET PICKLE SLICES

HOT CHICKEN SANDWICHES

1 soft roll
1 Baked Chicken Thigh (recipe follows), hot

Cut the roll in half and pull out a bit of the bottom half. Shred the chicken and stuff the roll. Spoon a bit of the hot pan juices over all.

BAKED CHICKEN THIGHS

Here is my simple method of cooking chicken. I skin these before eating them and remove the bone. And I degrease and save the pan juices.

6 medium chicken thighs
Salt and black pepper to taste

Preheat the oven to 400 degrees.

Salt and liberally pepper the chicken pieces, then place them, skin side up, in an ovenproof dish into which they fit very snugly (this keeps them from drying out). Make sure the skin is stretched to cover all the meat. Bake for 20 minutes, then turn off oven. Allow to remain in the oven (and continue to cook) in the residual heat for an additional 30 minutes.

———

TINY FRESH ASPARAGUS

SLICED FRESH TOMATOES

TINY FRESH ASPARAGUS

When the very thin asparagus first become available I always have at least one "pig out" meal of them. Nothing but lots of asparagus.

1 handful of pencil-thin asparagus
1 tablespoon unsalted butter
Salt and pepper to taste
Lemon slices
Ripe tomatoes, sliced

Bend the asparagus stalks to break off tough ends and discard ends. Place butter in a skillet. Wash asparagus tops, then put them on the butter with just the water that clings to them. Cover tightly and cook over high heat, shaking pan often, for 5 minutes. If not quite done, give them another minute. Do not overcook.

Remove asparagus to a plate and pour the pan juices over all. Add salt and pepper. Serve with lemon slices and tomatoes.
Serves 1

ENGLISH MUFFIN PIZZAS

These are so easy to do, you can't miss with them.

- 1 English muffin, split
- 3 or 4 teaspoons good olive oil
- 4 or more heaping teaspoons grated jack, cheddar, fontina, aged asiago, or Alpine Lace cheese
- Black pepper

Toast the English muffin lightly on both sides. Place cut side up on a baking sheet (or sheet of foil). Drizzle with a couple teaspoons of olive oil, then sprinkle the cheese evenly over each half. Run under the broiler until cheese has melted and begins to bubble. Cut each half in two (this is hot). Drizzle more olive oil over all and top with a generous grind of black pepper.

Eat with black olives and roasted peppers.

Serves 1

BLACK OLIVES

I've learned in my travels that even when they are not available in bulk, Greek and Italian black olives (I'm not referring to those bland California canned ripe black olives) are often available in jars. These usually have no liquid with them so I dump them into a small bowl and add a crushed garlic clove and cover them with olive oil to restore them. You may also add a pinch of dried rosemary.

ROASTED PEPPERS

If I am just making these for myself, I never roast more than 2 — maybe 1 red and 1 yellow — because they are fairly perishable even when refrigerated.

Put bell peppers on a foil-lined cookie sheet and place them directly under the broiler. Leave them there until the skins turn black, then turn them with tongs. When all sides are black, remove them to a small paper bag and fold shut. (Bagging the peppers while they cool steams them and makes them easier to peel.) Leave for 15 to 20 minutes before picking off the skin and removing the seeds.

Cut into wide strips and layer in a dish, covering each layer with olive oil. Top with a grind of black pepper. Allow to come to room temperature before eating.

———

English Muffin Pizza; Bean, Bacon, Potato, and Red Pepper Soup; Lettuce Risotto; and Hot Turkey Patty Sandwich

BEAN, BACON, POTATO, AND RED PEPPER SOUP

I have soup at least three times a week and I make it out of anything handy. Here is one of my favorites. You may make this soup with sweet potatoes and other types of dried beans. Use whatever you've got.

¼	pound hickory-cured slab bacon, cut into ⅜-inch dice (do not remove rind)
1	tablespoon unsalted butter
½	small onion, diced small
½	large carrot, scraped and diced small
1	small celery rib, diced small
4	cups chicken stock
¾	teaspoon salt
¼	teaspoon white pepper
2	medium to large leeks, white part only, washed and cut into ½-inch circles
2	medium to large potatoes, about 1 pound, peeled and cut into 1-inch cubes
¾	large red bell pepper, diced
1	10½-ounce can white kidney beans, drained and lightly rinsed

In a large pot cover the bacon dice with water and simmer for 5 minutes. Drain and press dry in paper towels. Wipe out pot and return bacon. Fry until golden and crisp over medium-low heat, about 4 minutes. Remove to a paper towel and reserve. Discard all rendered fat except 2 teaspoons; add the butter and return to heat. When foamy, add the onion, carrot, and celery. Sauté until brown, about 5 minutes. Add the chicken stock, reserved bacon, salt, and pepper. Simmer, skimming foam, for 5 minutes. Add leeks and potatoes. Simmer 5 minutes then add the red bell pepper. Continue cooking, skimming as needed, until potatoes are just tender when pierced with the point of a knife, about 5 more minutes. Add beans and simmer for another minute or so. Correct seasoning, turn off the heat, and allow the soup to sit 30 minutes before serving.

Serves 6

HOT TURKEY PATTY SANDWICH

Ball park mustard really does make a difference here.

2	slices country white bread
	Mayonnaise and yellow mustard to taste
1	Grace's Turkey Patty (recipe follows)
	Lettuce
	Dill pickle, sliced

Spread the bread lightly with mayonnaise and mustard. Add the patty, some lettuce, and slices of dill pickle.

GRACE'S TURKEY PATTIES

Grace Monroe, who has worked for me for years now, makes these wonderfully flavorful patties from ground turkey meat for a quick lunch or dinner. Good hot or at room temperature. And, of course, they may also be made with ground chicken.

1¼	pounds ground turkey
½	cup finely chopped onion
½	cup finely chopped green bell pepper
½	teaspoon black pepper
2	cups chicken stock reduced to ⅓ cup
1½	tablespoons vegetable oil

Combine the turkey, onion, green bell pepper, black pepper, and stock. Mix well and form into 6 patties.

Heat oil in a medium skillet and brown patties quickly on both sides over medium heat. Reduce heat and continue cooking until done through, about 15 minutes.

Makes 6 patties

LETTUCE RISOTTO

Having been brought up to think that when rice is properly cooked the individual grains are tender and fall separately onto the plate, I'm not one of those people who swoon over risotto. I got used to it, but never loved it until Barbara Kafka came along. Her microwave method produces a wonderfully light dish. I use her basic recipe and add to it anything I have in the fridge—from lettuce or mustard greens to beans.

When I make it for a solo dinner, I have no other accompaniment but a slice of good bread and a glass of wine. When I make it for company, I add prosciutto to dress it up (see page 146).

1	tablespoon unsalted butter
1	tablespoon olive oil
¼	cup minced onion
½	cup Arborio rice
1½	cups plus 2 tablespoons chicken stock, heated
¾	teaspoon salt
	Black pepper to taste
½	cup tightly packed shredded lettuce leaves
	Freshly grated Parmesan cheese (optional)

Place the butter and oil in an 8- or 9-inch ovenproof dish. Cook, uncovered, on high in a microwave oven for 2 minutes. Stir in onion and cook another 2 minutes. Stir in rice and cook for 2 minutes. Stir in chicken stock, salt, and pepper. Cook for 9 minutes. Stir in lettuce and cook for another 8 minutes. Allow to stand, uncovered, for another 5 minutes, stirring several times. Serve with a sprinkling of Parmesan cheese.

Serves 1

Index

OTHER LEE BAILEY TITLES FROM GRAMERCY BOOKS:

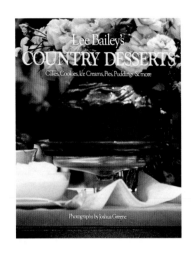 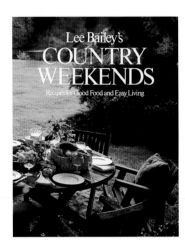 

LEE BAILEY'S COUNTRY DESSERTS

LEE BAILEY'S COUNTRY WEEKENDS

LEE BAILEY'S COUNTRY FLOWERS